Antislavery Materials at Bowdoin College

A Finding Aid

Angela M. Leonard
Editor

Bowdoin College
Brunswick, Maine
1992

This publication has been edited and compiled by Angela M. Leonard, consortium dissertation fellow and lecturer in history at Bowdoin College for 1990-1991, with students in History 336: The Abolitionist Tradition Reconsidered: Kristin L. Hall '91, Gregory J. Hostetter '91, Michael E. Libonati '91, Daniel J. Lind '91, Bruce C. Moses '91, John R. Nicholson, Jr. '91, Harriet H. Richards '92, and Sharma J. Simmons '94, and with the extensive research assistance of Annalisa M. Ravin '92, Jill M. DeTemple '93, Marie-France Anglade (SP), Dale F. Murray '91, and Peter J. Relic '93.

All copy photographs by Annalisa M. Ravin '92 except John Brown Russwurm photo on page vi.

This publication is funded by the Hawthorne-Longfellow Library, the Africana Studies Program, the Office of the Dean for Academic Affairs, the Bowdoin College Faculty Research Fund, and the Department of History.

Cover: Thomas Killion, *The U.S. and Africa*, 1991, wood engraving.

© Text copyright by the President and Trustees of Bowdoin College, 1991.
© Cover illustration copyright by Thomas C. Killion, 1991.
All rights reserved

Library of Congress Catalog Card Number: 92-70213
ISBN: 0-916606-22-8

Contents

List of Illustrations v
Foreword vii
Acknowledgments ix
Introduction xi
1. Bowdoin Resource Facilities 1
2. Bowdoin Alumni 5
3. Bowdoin Student Organizations 27
4. Bowdoin Overseers, Trustees, and Presidents 29
5. Bowdoin Faculty Members and Administrators 39
6. Maine Antislavers 41
7. Major Figures in Antislavery 49
Appendix A. Bowdoin and Maine Antislavers:
    General Holdings 61
Appendix B. Journals, Church and Society Reports,
    and Monographs 69
Appendix C. Samuel and William Pitt
    Fessenden Letters 89
Bibliography 91
Index 95
Notes on Compilers 99

List of Illustrations

John Brown Russwurm	vi
Memorial Hall and Bronze Plaque	3
John Appleton	4
Winslow Homer, *Expulsion of Negroes and Abolitionists from Tremont Temple, Boston, on December 3, 1860.*	26
John White Chickering	40
Oliver Otis Howard	40
Thomas Cogswell Upham	60
William Smyth	60
John Searle Tenney	68
Leonard Woods	68
Alpheus Spring Packard	90
William Pitt Fessenden	90
John Parker Hale	90

John Brown Russwurm (1799-1851), Class of 1826, Bowdoin College's first African-American graduate, publisher, editor, governor of the colony of Maryland, Liberia.

Foreword

It is a cliché to say that the history of an event or movement is the cumulative evidence drawn from the oral and written records of those who witnessed it and participated in it. The Abolitionist movement in the mid-nineteenth century attracted men and women whose conscience demanded they take a stand against an evil institution that legalized enforced servitude for millions of fellow human beings. While Bowdoin College could not be described as a hotbed of reformist zealots, it was indeed a place whose ambient permitted, indeed encouraged, men and women of conscience to voice their opposition to powerfully entrenched institutions such as slavery, which they saw as the embodiment of evil. That Bowdoin men and women were involved in the movement, and that evidence of the involvement was available in the library's Special Collections, has always been acknowledged. However, it took the efforts of the instructor and students enrolled in History 336 in the 1991 spring term, along with student research assistants, to bring to light its true extent.

The project, led by Angela M. Leonard, consortium dissertation fellow and instructor in history for 1990-1991, was intended to identify primary sources in the manuscript holdings of Special Collections for the study of the antislavery movement. The success of the project is demonstrated in the pages that follow. The manuscript collections yielded a quantity of material on the subject startling even to those who thought they were very familiar with its contents. The students in the course, whose names are cited elsewhere in these pages, spent many hours combing through files of letters and documents. Time ran out before their enthusiasm flagged.

The information within these covers will be invaluable to scholars and researchers who want to study roots of the antislavery movement. Laid out for them is a pathway to rich and varied sources of material recorded by many of those who actively participated in the movement. The students uncovered many items left by names not well known in the prominent histories of the movement. Their discoveries, which are printed in this guide, reaffirm the importance of collecting and preserving contemporary records for the benefit of those who at some future time will seek a new vision of their heritage.

>Arthur Monke
>Bowdoin College Librarian

Acknowledgments

A host of Bowdoin colleagues have facilitated the realization of this reference tool. Members of the class of History 336: The Abolitionist Tradition Reconsidered are profoundly indebted to Dianne M. Gutscher, curator of Special Collections, and Susan B. Ravdin, Special Collections assistant. Their enthusiasm for this project translated into an outpouring of assistance, without which much of our effort would have been futile.

It is especially important to note that Arthur Monke, the college librarian, was the first administrator to corroborate and validate the importance of this document for publication. The distribution of this guide was also made possible by the library staff under the supervision of another supportive colleague, Judith R. Montgomery, assistant librarian. Mr. Monke's support was soon followed by that of Associate Professor Randolph Stakeman, director of the Africana Studies Program. A special thanks is extended to him for his encouragement and for donating support to this project under the auspices of his office. I am immensely grateful to Lucie G. Teegarden, associate director of College Relations, Susan L. Ransom, editor, and other members of Bowdoin College's Office of College Relations, especially Craig C. Cheslog '93, for their expertise in overseeing the publication of this guide. Alfred H. Fuchs, dean of the faculty, helped tremendously to ease some of the burdens associated with a project of this magnitude.

Bowdoin's nineteenth-century memorials were brought to my attention by Patricia M. Anderson, author of *The Architecture of Bowdoin College* (Bowdoin College, 1988). Philip C. Beam, Henry Johnson Professor of Art and Archaeology Emeritus, through informal chats at Prout's Neck and through his canon of Homer scholarship, adjusted my intellectual appreciation of Winslow Homer's nineteenth-century depictions of "Negroes" and expanded my knowledge of Bowdoin's holdings of practically all (214) of Homer's wood engravings. In their special ways, Katharine J. Watson, director of the Bowdoin College Museum of Art; Louis D. Johnston, assistant professor of economics; Marilyn Reizbaum, associate professor of English; Franklin G. Burroughs, Jr., professor of English; Allen Wells, associate professor of history; Charles C. Calhoun, editor of *Bowdoin* magazine; and especially Thomas C. Killion, assistant professor of history, have contributed to this project.

In addition to the students named on the title page, the following students have worked assiduously—in some cases up to fifteen hours each—as research assistants to help bring this interminable project to a screeching halt: Jason B. Brown '91, Ruth Ann Gould '92, Vincent P. Jacks, Jr. '91, Doug J. Jorgenson '91, Alexander E. McCray '93, and Robert H. Smith '91. Their remuneration was made possible by an award from the Bowdoin Faculty Research Fund, and generously by the Department of History through the approval of the chair, Professor Paul L. Nyhus.

As the list of compilers indicates, this began as a collaborative project within the parameters of History 336: The Abolitionist Tradition Reconsidered. It has blossomed into a college-wide production with many named and unnamed persons offering an informative note or two. Members of History 336 join me in thanking all who have shared in our obsessive and tenacious trek through Bowdoin's literary depository of learning.

Introduction

Bowdoin College was one of the first institutions of higher learning in the United States to graduate a man of color. Ever since John Brown Russwurm received a baccalaureate degree from Bowdoin in 1826, the school has been revered as an institution which is steeped in the nation's founding principles of liberty and democracy. The sizable assortment of antislavery artifacts at Bowdoin suggests that before, during, and after the Civil War, antislavery was definitely an intellectual curiosity throughout the College, as evidenced by the library catalogues of the College's literary societies (Peucinian and Athenaean).

The college community had in its midst during the nineteenth century individuals who were representative of one or more antislavery propositions: colonization (Negro emigration to Liberia, Haiti, Canada, etc.); Christian conversion (missionary proseltyzing to the "African heathen"); Garrisonian moral suasion, also called "immediatism"; political agitation (Liberty Party, Free Soil, and Republican Party platforms); and Reconstruction and post-Reconstruction (freedmen missionary schools and Negro suffrage). The annotated individual profiles indicate that most Bowdoin antislavers manifested their reformist temperament after they reached full adult status (i.e. after graduation), or after they had securely settled into professional careers, frequently as members of the clergy (usually Congregationalists, fewer Methodists, few to no Baptists, even though there were local Maine Baptist Anti-Slavery Societies), judges (Supreme Court and District), principals of local academies (especially in Hallowell), politicians (more Republicans than Democrats), and merchants (ironically, in the seafaring trade and the cotton industry).

The biographical glimpses of the persons featured in this guide also reveal that most antislavers were issue-oriented, which often cast a shadow of ambiguity upon them, and which will (and already has) led many to question their commitment to the cause. Blatantly hypocritical figures I have omitted, but some individuals are included here who were considered "moderate" on the emancipation of slaves, for instance, members of the Maine Union in Behalf of the Colored Race.

This guide comprises individual biographical profiles of antislavers who have some affiliation with Bowdoin. While the complete biographical entries are of Bowdoin graduates and nongraduates, professors, Overseers, Trustees, and administrators, this work also features local Maine residents and a sampling of national antislavery figures who, like Bowdoin alumni, have been linked to antislavery through Bowdoin Special Collections. Unless otherwise indicated, the manuscripts and other documents cited are all housed in Special Collections.

A word about the entries themselves. Each individual is profiled once, and cross-references are provided when individuals fall into more than one category. Bowdoin graduates who are linked to antislavery only through secondary sources are cross-referenced with Bowdoin graduates, but the full profile appears in Appendix A. The most complete entries are of antislavers who have some affiliation with Bowdoin, for they are the principal focus of this booklet. Therefore, immediately following their names, printed in **bold,** are degrees, dates the degrees were received, and/or positions held at the College. Immediately following the biographical data are abbreviations of the sources consulted. These abbreviations refer to titles listed in the Bibliography. (Sources not cited in the Bibliography are footnoted.) The section of the entry entitled References lists both published and unpublished holdings in Bowdoin's Special Collections that refer to the individual's position on antislavery. Entries under Section 6: Major Figures in Antislavery are not biographically complete because information on these persons is relatively easy to obtain. Therefore, the References section in this chapter stresses primary documents on these individuals that Bowdoin owns and that may be retrieved from one or more of the large collections of personal papers. The actual documents cited consist of published and unpublished materials—books, letters, speeches, pamphlets, recordings, paintings, etc., which are housed at one or more facilities or offices at Bowdoin. I have included published material that is rare, out-of-print, or otherwise difficult to find.

Most of the individuals listed in this document were initially identified as Maine antislavers through Austin Willey's *History of Antislavery in State and Nation* (1886). Willey's text, essentially a history of antislavery in Maine, connects over fifty persons to this reform. Edward Schriver's *Go Free: The Antislavery Impulse in Maine,* Calvin Montague Clark's *American Slavery and Maine*

Congregationalists, the anti-slavery chapter in Burrage's *History of the Baptists in Maine,* as well as signatures from several locally derived antislavery petitions (obtained from the Maine State Library), have identified local participants in antislavery. Only a modicum of energy has been invested in locating material on individuals unconnected with Bowdoin. Such an endeavor would fill another challenging semester or even full-year class project.

To avoid misleading the zealous and expeditious researcher, it should be underscored that not all of the citations link individual figures directly to antislavery. In some instances, one may only glean the likelihood of a subject's involvement in antislavery activity by his expression of some liberal leaning in a letter to someone else associated with antislavery. Special Collections and other resource facilities at the College, therefore, should be approached as a first step.

This is not a guide to "abolition" materials, even though it germinated in a course entitled The Abolitionist Tradition Reconsidered. Traditionally, historians have placed abolitionists and abolitionism between 1830 and 1860/70, as well as the accompanying advocacy of "immediatism" as the preferred position on emancipation. In reality, British Quakers called for the immediate freedom of African slaves as early as the 1600s. Oddly, there are relatively few studies in the huge canon of antislavery literature that conceptually trace the continuity of abolitionist thought from British antislavery. This document does not seek to provoke semantic debate, but to encourage historical research. Consequently, I have opted to use the widely accepted and chronologically broader term "antislavery," especially since it is generally agreed that abolitionists were antislavers but not all antislavers were "immediatists."

This document is not submitted as exhaustive; it is merely a fraction of the tip of a murky iceberg. Amazingly, it is the product of only one semester's work. I have judiciously selected certain collections to leave un-mined for whoever decides to expand or simply continue this challenging and public service-oriented project. Begging for a more extensive examination are the Fessenden family papers (see section 7), the Edward Abbott Memorial Collection, the Hale-King papers, the Joshua Chamberlain Papers, the papers of Oliver Otis Howard's brothers, Charles and Rowland, and the papers of local merchant Neal

Dow, to mention only a few. Nevertheless, I proudly present this guide as a modest and preliminary step toward uncovering gems at the College on this significant reform movement in nineteenth-century American history.

Angela M. Leonard
Brunswick, Maine 1991

1
Bowdoin Resource Facilities

HAWTHORNE-LONGFELLOW LIBRARY
(OPEN STACKS)

Newspapers: The library owns complete sets on microfilm of two Maine abolition newspapers—*The Advocate of Freedom* and the *Liberty Standard* (7/12/1841-8/31/1848). Also on seventeen reels of microfilm is a complete assemblage of Black Abolitionists Newspapers. Bowdoin College has recently acquired this collection of documents, mostly dated from 1830 through 1865, with a few prior to 1830 that have no date. The individual items in this collection are letters to the editor, editorials, and poems, notices, and advertisements. Some serials included are: Henry Bibbs's *Voice of the Fugitive*, William Days's *Aliened American*, Frederick Douglass's *North Star*, Samuel Cornish's *Weekly Advocate and Colored American*, Stephen Myer's *Northern Star and Freeman's Advocate*, David Ruggles's *Mirror of Liberty*, James McCune Smith's *Weekly Anglo-African*, and Thomas Van Renssaelaer's *Ram Horn*. The library also owns other antislavery society newspapers, journals and reports. See Appendix B.

The Alpha Room: This storage space appears to be a midway station for some rare books that fall short of the cutoff for inclusion in Special Collections—1820 for imprints, generally, and 1835 for Maine imprints. Some books in the Alpha Room are duplicates of items found elsewhere at the College; there are also oversized tattered folios and valuable nineteenth-century publications (like Antislavery Tracts—publications of the American Antislavery Society) that require controlled circulation. Alpha books are listed in the card catalogue but not all of them are in the online catalogue.

HAWTHORNE-LONGFELLOW LIBRARY
(SPECIAL COLLECTIONS)

This depository is located on the third floor. To find resources here, you must examine at least five files: 1) MSS index; 2) Manuscripts file; 3) Main Entry holdings; 4) black binder of speeches, pamphlets, etc., arranged alphabetically by author; and 5) black binder cross-referencing individual collections. If your subject is a member of the Board of Trustees or a professor, you should also consult the following directories: 1) Biographical Files; 2) College Records; and 3) Reports of the Visiting Committee.

Special Collections owns several sets of personal papers, records of area societies, and antislavery pamphlets which will prove invaluable to the researcher of antislavery. They deserve singular attention and are discussed in Sections 6 and 7 and Appendix B.

BOWDOIN COLLEGE MUSEUM OF ART

The Bowdoin College Museum of Art owns all but about seven of Winslow Homer's wood engravings. Out of the 214 wood engravings by Homer in the museum, there are approximately ten that depict blacks in the nineteenth century—before, during, and after the Civil War. The museum also owns at least two original early nineteenth-century portraits of blacks (*Portrait of a Gentleman,* circa 1830, and *Coxacie Tom,* circa 1810) by unknown artists. Although these items are available for viewing by appointment (they are not always on public display), some are featured in the following publications: *The Portrayal of the Negro in American Painting* (Bowdoin College Museum of Art, 1964), *Winslow Homer's Images of Blacks: The Civil War and Reconstruction Years* (Austin: University of Texas Press, 1988), and *Winslow Homer's Magazine Engravings,* by Philip C. Beam, Henry Johnson Professor of Art and Archaeology Emeritus and former director of the museum (Harper & Row, 1979). Of particular relevance is Homer's engraving "Expulsion of Negroes and Abolitionists from Tremont Temple, Boston, Mass. on Dec. 3, 1860," which was published in Harper's Weekly, Dec. 15, 1860.

MEMORIALS

Fessenden Room: This room is located on the second floor of Hawthorne-Longfellow Hall. It contains portraits of **General Samuel Fessenden**, his sons **William Pitt Fessenden** 1823 and **Samuel Clement Fessenden** 1834 (all three were Overseers), and William Pitt's son, **Samuel Fessenden** 1861, who was killed in the Civil War.

Memorial Hall in 1887 with its original doorway.

Memorial Hall and Pickard Theater: As you enter this building you are greeted in the lobby by several bronze plaques commissioned to sustain the memory of Bowdoin alumni who fought on the Union side in the Civil War. Bowdoin men who fought with the Confederacy are listed on a plaque above the left-hand staircase. The history of this building is also pertinent, for Professor William Smyth, Bowdoin's and Brunswick's most identifiable antislaver, almost single-handedly realized the construction of Memorial Hall. From 1865 to 1867, he crusaded for its erection by raising $20,000 for that purpose (Anderson 33-37). Among the names engraved on the plaques are those of two

The bronze plaques in the lobby of Pickard Theater list Bowdoin men who fought with the Union side in the Civil War.

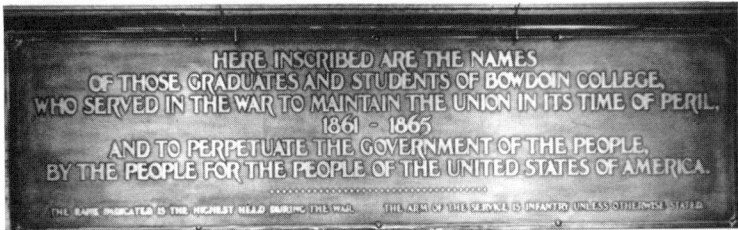

of Smyth's sons, **William Henry Smyth** 1856, and **Edward Beecher Smyth,** who attended Bowdoin in 1850-1851, as well as other famous Bowdoin names, among them **Oliver Otis Howard** 1850, **Thomas Brackett Reed** 1860, and **Samuel Fessenden** and **Alpheus Spring Packard, Jr.**, both 1861.

Peucinian Room: A room dedicated to the Peucinian Society is in the basement of Sills Hall.

John Brown Russwurm African American Center (Africana Studies Program): Legend has it that the building memorialized as the John Brown Russwurm African American Center was a stop on the "underground railroad," though the information on this house does not unequivocally prove the legend. Built in 1827 by Samuel Melcher III, the dwelling was initially a two-family house. Professor William Smyth lived on one side, and his life-long friend Professor Alpheus Spring Packard lived on the other. The house is now home to the Africana Studies Program and a culturally focused library with a card catalog. Although this depository duplicates some materials in Hawthorne-Longfellow, it contains the only copy available on campus of certain items. It is not an archival depository.

John Appleton (1804-1891), Class of 1822.

2
Bowdoin Alumni

A very small segment of the Bowdoin student population was involved in antislavery activities. A Bowdoin Colonization Society existed, but little is known about this organization other than a bookplate reference. The following graduates, nongraduates, and honorary degree recipients have been identified as having expressed antislavery sentiments.

Aaron Chester Adams (A.B. 1836, Overseer 1866-71) *Birth:* April 7, 1815 Bangor, ME; *Death:* June 29, 1849 Wethersfield, CT; *Additional Education:* studied at Lane Seminary, graduated Bangor Seminary 1839; *Career:* Clergy, Gardiner, ME 1839-41; Gorham, ME 1842-45; Montclair, NJ; High Street Congregational Church Auburn, ME, and Malden, MA 1858-67; Congregational Church Wethersfield, CT 1867-79; Thompson, CT 1880-86; *Family:* married Harriet S. Johnson Aug. 14, 1839; two sons and two daughters; *Professional and Social Affiliations:* Phi Beta Kappa (Bowdoin); member of United States Christian Commission during the Civil War. (GCB, 71; Clark, 188-89)

References: Biographical File: unidentified newspaper clipping mentions "Adams's vigorous Philippics for freedom in the old anti-slavery days"; and Alumni Pamphlet: *An Address to Abolitionists of the Methodist Episcopal Church, Boston,* delivered to the Anti-Slavery Society of Maine Annual Conference (Boston: Reid and Rand, 1843), re: that the doctrine of Methodism finds slaveholding intolerable. See entry on **David Thurston** for Adams's tribute to him.

John Albion Andrew (A.B. 1837) *Birth:* May 31, 1818 Windham, ME; *Death:* Oct. 30, 1867; *Additional Education:* LL.D. Amherst 1861, LL.D. Harvard 1861; *Career:* Lawyer, Boston, MA 1840-67; Massachusetts Legislature 1859; Governor of MA 1861-66; *Professional and Social Affiliations:* President, American Unitarian Association; President, New England Historical and Genealogical Society, 1866-67; Overseer, Harvard 1867; Trustee, M.I.T.; Phi Beta Kappa, Athenaean Society, Delta Kappa Epsilon (all Bowdoin). (GCB, 79)

References: Alumni Pamphlets: *Valedictory Address of his Excellency John A. Andrew to the Two Branches of the Legislature of Massachusetts,* Jan. 4, 1866 (Boston: Wright & Potter, 1866), re: stresses equality under the law, ratification of the antislavery amendment, Africans are people and are, therefore, protected under the law, and they also need and deserve representatives in the Legislature; "Selection" in *Sword and the Pen* (Boston) Dec. 7, 1881; there are several pamphlets in the Biographical Files: *Discourse delivered before New England Historic-Genealogical Society on the Life and Character of Hon. John Albion Andrew* by Rev. Elias Nason (Boston: The Society, 1868); *Memorial Address: Delivered before the John Albion Andrew Monument Association at Hingham, October 8, 1875* (Boston: Rockwell & Churchill, 1875), Horace Binney Sargent mentions that he procured the defense of the quintessential abolitionist John Brown and aided his family, prepared for war before Sumter, and defended free speech, 100% supporter of Lincoln; *Unveiling of the Statue of Gov. John A. Andrew at the State House,* Tuesday, Feb. 14, 1871 (Boston: Wright & Potter).

John Appleton (A.B. 1822, A.M. 1825, LL.D. 1860, Overseer 1868-70, Trustee 1870-91) *Birth:* July 12, 1804 New Ipswich, NH; *Death:* Feb. 7, 1891; *Additional Education:* studied law with George F. Farley, Esq. (New Ipswich, NH) and Nathan Dane Appleton, Esq. (Alfred, ME, Bowdoin 1813); *Career:* Assistant teacher in Dummer Academy (Byfield, MA) for a few months immediately after Bowdoin, and for a short time in Watertown, MA; Lawyer (admitted to the Bar 1826 in Amherst, NH) Dixmont, ME 1826, Sebec, ME 1827-32, Bangor, ME (partner with Hon. Elisha H. Allen, later with John B. Hill, and later with his cousin Moses Appleton) 1832-52; Reporter of Decisions 1841-42 (prepared two volumes for the press); Justice, Maine Supreme Court, 1852-1862; Chief Justice, 1862-83; Lecturer of Medical Jurisprudence, 1870-71; *Professional and Social Affiliations:* Phi Beta Kappa, Peucinian Society (both Bowdoin); *Family:* nephew of second president of Bowdoin, **Jesse Appleton**; married twice, Sarah N. Allen 1834-74; Annie V. Greely 1876; five children, two sons attended Bowdoin: **General John Francis** 1860 (served in the Civil War), and **Frederick H.** 1864. (GCB, 52; Willey, 120)

References: See "Opinion of Judges Appleton and [Edward] Kent" in *Opinions of the Several Justices of the S. J. Court, on the Constitutionality of the Personal Liberty Laws of the State of Maine*

(Augusta 1861, 19-32), in which Appleton contends that Maine's Personal Liberty Laws were not "repugnant" to and constitutionally in violation of the 1850 Fugitive Slave Law; maintained that the Dred Scott decision was not binding on the Maine Court.[1]

James Gillespie Blaine (LL.D. 1884) *Birth:* Jan. 31, 1830 W. Brownsville, PA; *Death:* Jan. 27, 1893 Washington, D.C. *Education:* A.B. Washington College 1847, A. M. Washington College, LL.D. Colby 1875, LL.D. Bates 1869; Career: Teacher, Pennsylvania School for the Blind 1852-54; editor, *Kennebec Journal* 1853-1858, Portland *Advertiser* 1858; *Kennebec Journal* 1860 but left again to reenter politics; Maine State Legislature (Republican) 1859-62; Speaker of State House 1861-62; member of Congress 1863-76; Speaker of U.S. House 1869-75; U.S. Senator 1876-81; Secretary of State 1881, 1889-92; *Professional and Social Affiliations:* Not a staunch abolitionist but vehemently opposed Hayes's "Compromise of 1877," Thaddeus Stevens and Roscoe Conkling, and he has interesting connections to members of the movement, such as **Luther Severence,** of whom he wrote a biography, and **William Lloyd Garrison,** who concurred with him against Hayes.[2] (GCB, 6; BDAC, 856)

References: Letter (July 25, 1865, Augusta, ME) in **Oliver Otis Howard** Papers recommending Brig. General H. G. Thomas,[3] an early advocate of "elevating the negro to a *man* in this war [Civil War]," for employment with the Freedmen's Bureau.[4] See also **William P. Frye** Alumni Pamphlets, especially a significant pamphlet by Frye entitled *Memorial Address Upon the Life and Character of the Late James G. Blaine* (Boston, 1893), which acknowledges Blaine's appeal for an antislavery party as a "protection party."

Elias Bond See entry under APPENDIX A.

Horatio Bridge (A.B. Maine Medical School 1825; A.M. 1828) *Birth:* April 8, 1806 Augusta, ME; *Death:* March 18, 1893; *Career:* Lawyer, Skowhegan, ME, Augusta, ME, 1828-1838 with **James Bradbury A.B. 1825, Medical School 1825, A.M. 1828, LL. D. 1872, Overseer 1850-60, Trustee 1860-1901**[5]; Purser, 1840 U.S. Navy for 16 years mostly at sea, appointed to USS Cyone 1838-1841—Sailed to African coast as part of U.S. squadron sent to enforce the anti-slave trade law 1841-1844; Sailed to African

7

coast and Mediterranean, USS Saratoga 1846-1848; Stationed at Portsmouth Naval Ship Yard 1849-1851; Appointed Chief of the Bureau of Provisions and Clothing USN 1854-1868; Appointed Chief Inspector of Clothing, USN 1869-1873 (under President **Franklin Pierce**[6]); retired to "The Moorings" family farm/estate in Athens, PA 1873-1893. *Family:* son of **James Bridge** (Trustee 1821-34), married to Charlotte Marshall of Boston 1846. (GCB, 56)

References: Personal journal, *Journal of an African Cruiser* (New York: Willey & Putnam), sketches of the Canaries, Cape de Verde, Liberia, Madeira, Sierra Leone, and other places on the west coast of Africa, edited by **Nathaniel Hawthorne** (Bridge's closest personal friend), 1845. See letter dated Oct. 30, 1890, from Bridge to **Professor George T. Little,** Bowdoin College librarian, inquires about **John Brown Russwurm** and any other "colored graduates of Bowdoin College." See also *Personal Recollections of Nathaniel Hawthorne.*

George Barrell Cheever (A.B. 1825) *Birth:* April 7, 1807 Hallowell, ME; *Death:* Oct. 1, 1890 Englewood, NJ; *Additional Education:* LL.D Andover Theological Seminary 1830, D.D. University of New York 1844; *Career:* Pastor, Howard Street Congregational Church, Salem, MA 1833-36; Pastor, Allen Street Presbyterian Church, NY 1839-44, 1846-47; Editor, in Scotland 1844, New York *Evangelist* 1846; Pastor, Church of the Puritans, NY 1846-1870; Religious writer, Englewood, NJ 1867-90; *Professional and Social Affiliations:* Phi Beta Kappa and Peucinian (both Bowdoin); member, American Anti-Slavery Society, later vice-president of the then dying American Anti-Slavery Society 1865-70. (GCB, 56)[7]

References: Alumni Pamphlets include the following written by Cheever and/or are about rights of blacks before and after the Civil War: "The Fire and Hammer of God's Word Against the Sin of Slavery," delivered at the Anniversary of the American Abolition Society, May 1858; "American Slavery, Demonstrations in Favor of Dr. Cheever in Scotland"; "Letter of Sympathy From Distinguished Clergymen and other Gentlemen"; "Speeches at Meetings in Edinburgh and Glasgow, by Drs. Candlish, Guthrie, Alexander, Buchanan, and Smyth"; "Statement of Dr. Cheever's Case by Rev. H. Batchelor"; "Letter of Dr. Guthrie to the Presbyterian," 1860; "Thaddeus Hyatt's Contributions To the Cause of Human Liberty and Constitutional Rights,"

Part III, Sermon delivered at the Church of the Puritans, NY, Sunday, May 20, 1860; "The Salvation of the Country Secured By Immediate Emancipation, A Discourse," delivered in the Church of the Puritans, Sabbath Evening, Nov. 10, 1861; "The Proposed Return into Egypt, And Its Consequences," A Discourse preached in Washington, D.C., Sabbath Evening, Feb. 15, 1863, in the Senate Chambers of the United States . . . on Numbers 14:4; "Rights of the Colored Race to Citizenship and Representation; And the Guilt and Consequences of Legislation Against Them," A Discourse Delivered in the Hall of Representatives of the United States in Washington, D.C., May 29, 1864, Pastor of the Church of Puritans in the city of New York; "A Change in Administration For the Security of the Government, A Christian Duty and a National Necessity," at the Fremont Ratification Meeting, in the Church of the Puritans, on Monday Evening, July 11, 1864; "Protest Against the Robbery of the Colored Race By the Proposed Amendment of the Constitution," 1866; "Impartial Suffrage, A Right; And the Infamy of the Revolution Against It in the Proposed Amendment of the Constitution," 1866. Available in the circulation collection is *The Guilt of Slavery and the Crime of Slaveholding, Demonstrated from the Hebrew and Greek Scriptures* (New York: Smith & McDougal, 1860)[8]; Cheever is also cited in **Horatio Bridge**'s *Personal Recollections of Nathaniel Hawthorne*. Bridge states, "Another of the remaining members of the class (Bowdoin 1825) was Rev. Dr. George B. Cheever (the early and able leader in the cause of abolition and temperance), who attained high eminence as a theologian" (19).

Henry T. Cheever (A.B. 1834) *Birth:* Feb. 6, 1814 Hallowell, ME; *Death:* Feb. 13, 1897; *Additional Education:* Bangor Theological Seminary 1839; *Career:* Correspondent of *New York Evangelist* from South Seas and Sandwich Islands 1842; Religious writer, 1840-52; Pastor, Broadway Church, Norwich, CT 1846; Pastor, Congregational Church, Lodi, NJ 1847-48; Pastor, Chrystie Street Congregational Church, New York 1848; Literary Service, 1849-1852; Pastor, Congregational Church, Greenport, Long Island, NY 1852-55; Westbrook, CT 1855-56; Pastor, Congregational Church, Jewett City 1856-61; S. Royalston, MA 1862-63; Fitchburg, MA 1863-64; Pastor, Mission Chapel Church, Worcester, MA 1864-1873; Literary work 1873-97; *Professional and Social Affiliations:* Phi Beta Kappa and Peucinian (both Bowdoin); organizer and secretary, Church Anti-Slavery Society (Worcester, MA) 1858-1865 (disbanded in 1865); *Family:* brother of **George Cheever**; married Jane Tyler in 1857; five daughters. (Cleaveland, 455-56; GCB, 67)

References: Alumni Pamphlets: "Constitution of The Church Anti-Slavery Society of the United States Declaration of Principles," December 20, 1858; "A Tract for the Times, On the Question, Is it Right to Withhold Fellowship From Churches or From Individuals That Tolerate or Practise Slavery?" Read by Appointment Before the Congregational Ministers' Meeting, of New London County, CT, 1859; Church Anti-Slavery Society Convention at Worcester, 1859, "Address to the People of the United States in Behalf of the National Reform League."

Edward Francis Cutter (A.B. 1828, Medical School 1828, A.M. 1831, D.D. 1871, Overseer 1852-80) *Birth:* Jan. 20, 1810 Portland, ME; *Death:* March 27, 1880 Charleston, SC; *Additional Education:* Studied at Andover Theological Seminary 1831; *Career:* Clergy (ordained 1833), First Church of Warren 1833-46, North Congregational Church of Belfast, ME 1846-55, First Congregational Church of Beardstown, IL 1857-59, Rockland 1863-72; Resided in Belfast 1859-63, 1873-80; Editor, *Christian Mirror* (succeeded **Rev. Asa Cummings** until April 1, 1857; *Professional and Social Affiliations:* Phi Beta Kappa and Peucinian Society (both Bowdoin); Member, Maine Union in Behalf of the Colored Race; *Family:* married Mary E. Sellaw; five children; son of **Levi Cutler, Overseer 1818-56.** (Clark, 60-62 ; GCB, 60)

References: Biographical Files; Alumni Pamphlets: *Eulogy on Lincoln, delivered, Rockland, ME, by request of Citizens,* pedestals Lincoln as "a man of the people" who redeemed the "poor bondmen. . . from the lash and the chain," and promises newly appointed Pres. Andrew Johnson the same reverence if he proves to be a "worker for the Union and Freedom, as Abraham Lincoln."

William Cutter See entry under APPENDIX A.

Philip Eastman (A.B. 1820, A.M. 1823, Overseer 1831-64, Trustee 1864-69) *Birth:* Feb. 5, 1799 Chatham, NH; *Death:* Aug. 7, 1869; *Additional Education:* studied law first in office of Stephen Chase, Esq., of Fryeburg, then in office of Hon. Nicholas Baylies of Montpelier, VT, later in office of Judah Dana of Fryeburg; *Career:* Lawyer, North Yarmouth 1823-36, Harrison 1836-47, Saco

1847-69; Chairman, County Commissioners of Cumberland County, 1831-37; Maine State Senate 1840 (also chairman of Committee on the Revision of the Statutes of the State), 1842; commissioned under the Treaty of Washington of 1842 to locate Grants and Possessory Claims to Settlers on the St. John and Aroostook Rivers 1843-44; *Professional and Social Affiliations:* Phi Beta Kappa and Peucinian (both Bowdoin); secretary of the newly formed Maine Colonization Society, 1855; *Family:* married Mary Ambrose 1827; four sons, three daughters. (GCB, 51; Clark, 176)

References: Biographical File: Letter to Hon. Robert Dunlop, Feb. 8, 1845 (Harrison, ME) re: admission of slave territory and representation of slaves in Congress.

John Wallace Ellingwood See entry under APPENDIX A.

John Fairfield (A.M. [Hon.] 1845) *Birth:* Jan. 30, 1797 Saco, ME; *Death:* Dec. 24, 1847 Washington, D.C.; *Additional Education:* studied law under Judge Shepley; *Career:* Lawyer (admitted to the Bar 1826), Biddeford, ME (partnership with George Thatcher), Saco, ME; Report to the State Supreme Court 1832; U. S. Congress (Democrat) 1835-38; Governor 1839, 1840, 1842-43; ME State Senate 1840; U.S. Senate 1843-47; *Family:* married Annie Paine 1825; nine children. (GCB, 548; Schriver, 47-48)

References: Biographical File: Letter from Jason Whitman (brother) informs Fairfield of the antislavery (as well as anti-abolitionist) biographical profile of him that Whitman painted for the Savannah, GA, newspapers.[9] See *The Letters of John Fairfield...*, ed. Arthur G. Staples (Lewiston, ME: Lewiston Journal Co., 1922), 51-54, 173-74, 334-35.

Joseph Palmer Fessenden (A.B. 1818) *Birth:* Oct. 24, 1792 Fryeburg, ME; *Death:* Feb. 13, 1861; *Career:* Clergy, Congregational Church, Arundel, ME (near Kennebunkport) 1820-29; South Bridgton, ME 1829-61; *Family:* married Phebe P. Beach 1819, no children; *Professional and Social Affiliations:* Peucinian Society (Bowdoin). (GCB, 50)

References: Alumni Pamphlets: "A Sermon Preached at North Bridgton at the Annual Meeting of the Union Conference" June 16, 1846 (Portland: F. A. and A. F. Gerrish, 1846), speaks of the U.S. war with Mexico as not only "a war of conquest, a war to gain possession of gold and silver mines, and rich cathedrals; but chiefly and above all, to obtain, by violence and fraud, a large and fruitful territory, for the perpetuation and wider extension of our hateful and heaven-accursed system of slavery. . . "(12). In Biographical Files, unidentified newspaper clipping states that Fessenden's addresses on antislavery and temperance to the people of York and Oxford counties "brought on him frequent opposition and reproach." In the Alumni Biographical Records File (Box 10, folder n) there is a manuscript fragment (three handwritten pages) re: the "injury" inflicted on the antislavery movement by pro-slavery publications of theologians and professors and "the profound insensibility which they have manifested in respect to the sins of American slavery"; but this same document commends "Mr' [William Lloyd] Garrison's antislavery clarion."

Samuel Clement Fessenden (A.B. 1834, A.M. 1837, Overseer 1854-67) *Birth:* March 7, 1815 New Gloucester, MA; *Death:* April 18, 1882; *Additional Education:* Studied Bangor Theological Seminary 1837; *Career:* Pastor, Congregation Church, Rockland, ME 1838-56; Editor, Lewiston, ME 1856-57; Lawyer, Rockland, ME 1858-65; Judge, Municipal Court, Rockland; U.S. Congress 1861-63; Examiner of U.S. Patent Office 1865-70; U.S. Consul, St. John, New Brunswick 1881-82 (resided in Stamford, CT, 1870-82); *Family:* son of **Samuel Fessenden, Overseer 1822-29.** (GCB, 67)

References: See "Lecture—Slavery Examined" (Delivered before the Anti-Slavery Society at East Minot, ME, Sept. 28, 1836); "The Slavery Question" (Jan. 22, 1862); and "Confiscation of Rebel Property" (May 22, 1862) in *Selections from the Speeches, Sermons, Addresses, etc. of Samuel Clement Fessenden* (New York: William P. Tomlinson, 1869)[10]; and see correspondence in the Fessenden and Thatcher Family collections.

William Pitt Fessenden (A.B. 1823, Medical School 1823, LL.D. 1858, Overseer 1843-60, Trustee 1860-69) *Birth:* Oct. 16, 1806 Boscawen, NH; *Death:* Sept. 8, 1869 Washington, D. C. (of "malarious influence"); *Additional Honorary Degree:* LL.D. Harvard 1864; *Career:* Lawyer, Bridgeton, ME 1827-29, Portland, ME 1829-32 (firm of his father, **Samuel Fessenden,** and Deblois), Bangor, ME 1833-35; 1832-33 (partnership with William Willis, Esq.); Maine State Legislature (Portland) 1832, 1839, 1845, 1846, 1853, 1854; U.S. Congress 1841-1843; U.S. Senator 1843, 1845,

1854-1864, 1865-69[11]; Chairman of the Senate Finance Committee 1854-60; Secretary of Treasury 1864-65; *Family:* illegitimate son of **General Samuel Fessenden**; brother of **Samuel Clement Fessenden**; married 1832 Ellen Maria, daughter of James Deering; one daughter and four sons, all sons received degrees from Bowdoin: **James Deering** A.B. 1852, **Francis** A.B. 1858, **Samuel** A.B. 1861, **William Howard** A.M. (honorary) 1865; *Professional and Social Affiliations:* President, General Alumni Association (Bowdoin) 1857-67; Phi Beta Kappa and Athenaean (both Bowdoin); remained "antislavery" throughout his career. (GCB, 54)[12]

References: Alumni Pamphlets: "Oration Deliverd Before the Young Men of Portland," July 4, 1827, asserts that America should follow Britain and emancipate slaves; "Speech on the Abolition of Slavery in the District of Columbia," April 1, 1862, perceives the Civil War as a fight to uphold the Constitution, not necessarily to end slavery, even though the government should abandon the institution; "Speech of W. P. F. Against the Repeal of the Missouri Prohibition, North of 36 30'. Delivered in the Senate of the United States, March 3, 1854, on the bill to establish Territorial Governments in Nebraska and Kansas," March 3, 1854, in which he airs his opposition to the Fugitive Slave Law, the admission of Missouri as a slave state, and the Kansas-Nebraska Bill, yet he affirms states' rights and property rights as secured by the Constitution; "Speech on the President's Message," 1856; "Speech on the Resolution Relating to the Admission of Senators and Representatives from the Confederate States," 1866. See also APPENDIX C.

Charles Freeman (A.B. 1812, A.M. 1815, Overseer 1846-47)
Birth: June 3, 1794 Portland, ME; *Death:* Sept. 19, 1853; *Additional Education:* Gorham Academy; studied law with Nicholas Emery, Esq., of Portland; studied for the ministry under Rev. Edmund Payson (Portland); *Career:* Lawyer, admitted to the Bar in Cumberland County 1815, Portland 1815-16; Clergy, licensed to preach by the Cumberland Association 1817, preached in Brunswick, Waterville, Camden, and Limington, ME; ordained in Limerick, ME 1820, Limerick 1820-53; *Family:* son of **Samuel Freeman, Overseer 1794-96, 1799-1819, Vice President of the Board 1813-15, President of the Board 1815-19, Treasurer, Trustee 1796-99**; married twice: Nancy Pierce (daughter of **Hon. Josiah Pierce, Bowdoin 1818**) 1822-25, one son, **Charles**

Marsden, Bowdoin A.B. 1845, A.M. 1848; married Salva Abbot, May 23, 1827, one son, Samuel, Bowdoin A.B. 1854. *Professional and Social Affiliations:* Peucinian (Bowdoin); one of ten Vice Presidents (represented York County), Maine Union in Behalf of the Colored Race; Trustee, Maine Congregational Charitable Society, also its Secretary 1829-48; Delegate from York, ME, at the organization of the General Conference of Maine (Congregational Churches); Corresponding Secretary, State Conference of Congregational Churches 1833-45; Vice President, Maine Domestic Missionary Society 1840-48. (GCB, 47; Clark, 62, 121)

References: Biographical File: "C.D.," author of Freeman biography "Familiar Recollections of Rev. Charles Freeman" for the *Evangelist* (n.d.), recalls attending an antislavery meeting with Freeman at the Friends Meeting House in Portland "when it was expected that the meeting would be molested by noise, if not by violence."

William Pierce Frye (A.B. 1850, A.M. 1853, LL.D. 1889, Overseer 1872-81, Trustee 1881-1911) *Birth:* Sept. 2, 1830 Lewiston, ME; *Death:* Aug. 8, 1911; *Honorary Degree:* LL.D Bates 1881; *Career:* Lawyer, Rockland, ME 1852-55, Lewiston 1855-1911; Register of Probate for Androscoggin County 1856-60; Mayor of Lewiston 1866-67; Maine State Legislature 1861-62, 1867; Maine Attorney General 1867-70; U.S. Congress 1871-81; U.S. Senate 1881-1911, President pro tem 1896-1911; *Professional and Social Affiliations:* Psi Upsilon and Peucinian Society (both Bowdoin). (GCB, 95)

References: Alumni Pamphlets: *Speech. . . Delivered in the United States Senate, Wednesday, April 20, 1881* (Washington, 1881), concerns the inequities by certain states in their expenditure of public funds to educate whites and blacks; *American Citizens must be Protected in their Right to Vote, Speech. . . in the Senate of the United States, Thursday, Dec. 11, 1890* (Washington, 1890), involves the role of Tammany in its collusion with Southern Democrats to fail to "secure to the trembling black citizen his right to the ballot" (15); "The Republican Party" in *Proceedings Fifth Annual Meeting of the Michigan Club, with a verbatim Report of Speeches at the Banquet on February 21st, 1890; Fifth Annual Report of the Secretary* (Detroit, MI: Winn & Hammond, 1890) (35-43), documents Frye's support of the "colored citizens" right to enfranchisement.

John Parker Hale (A.B. 1827) *Birth:* March 31, 1806 Rochester, NH; *Death:* Nov. 18, 1873; *Additional Education:* LL.D. Dartmouth 1861; *Career:* Law, Dover, NH; NH State Legislature, 1832; Speaker of House, 1846; U.S. District Attorney, ME 1834-1841; U.S. Congress, 1843-1845; U.S. Senate, 1847-53, 1855-65; Minister to the Court of Madrid 1865-69; Presidential nominee of the Liberty Party 1847 (withdrew nomination when Free Soil Party absorbed the Liberty Party in 1848 and favored Van Buren as a candidate), 1852; Presidential nominee of the Free Soil party (polled 50,000 votes); *Family:* married Lucy Lambert in 1832; two daughters; *Professional and Social Affiliations:* Phi Beta Kappa and Athenaean Society (both Bowdoin). (GCB, 59; Cleaveland, 369-70)

References: Biographical File: Alumni Pamphlets: *Speech. . . on the Abolition of Slavery in the District of Columbia, Delivered in the Senate, March 18, 1862; Debate in the Senate on the Protection of Property in the District of Columbia, From Houston's Senate Debate, April 20, 1848; Speech. . . on the State of the Union, Jan. 31, 1861; The Wrongs of Kansas, Speech. . . in the Senate, Feb. 1856; Massachusetts Liberty Convention, and Speech of. . .Together with his Letter Accepting his Nomination for the Presidency,* 1848; *Free Soil Document [No. 1]: Address and Resolutions of the Cleveland Convention, National Address at the Free Soil Convention, Held at Cleveland,* Sept. 24, 1851; *Remarks Made at a Democratic Meeting in Portsmouth, on the 7th of January 1845 in Defence of the Course of John P. Hale. . . in relation to the Annexation of Texas;* and *Speech of. . . on the Territorial Question, Delivered in the Senate. . . , March 19, 1850.*

James Hall (M.D. 1822) *Birth:* April 9, 1802 Cornish, NH; *Death:* Aug. 31, 1889 St. Denis (Baltimore) MD; *Career:* Physician, Clarmont, NH and Windsor, VT 1822-29, Liberia, Africa 1831-32; Governor, Maryland Colonization Society in Africa (Liberia) 1833-36; Merchant, Baltimore, MD; Editor, Maryland *State Colonization Journal* (housed in Maryland Historical Society) 1836; Baltimore manager of the Chesapeake and Liberia Trading Co.; General agent for the Maryland Colonization Society 1832-34; Commercial agent for American Colonization Society 1840-1861. (GCB, 437)

References: Correspondence: November 15, 1853, to A. Cleveland, Esq., Brooklyn NY, reference to **John Brown Russwurm**. More information on Russwurm in *Colonial Journal* #5, vol. 6. ("small monthly journal conducted by myself"). See also the *Baltimore American; The African Repository* (quarterly of the American Colonization Society), LXV (October 1889): 117; see also correspondence from G. W. S Hall to George Little, Aug. 13, 1889, St. Denis, MD; *New York Times*, Sept. 6, 1889, "Obituary: A Pioneer of Liberia"; also see the American Colonization Society's *Annual Reports* and the *Liberia Herald* (both at Hawthorne-Longfellow).[13]

Nathaniel Hawthorne (A.B. 1825, Medical School 1825, A.M. 1828) *Birth:* July 4, 1804 Salem, MA; *Death:* May 19, 1864 Plymouth, NH; *Career:* Author, Salem, MA 1825-38, 1846-50, Boston, MA 1838-42, Concord, MA 1842-46, 1852-53, 1860-64; U.S. Consul, Liverpool, England 1853-57; *Professional and Social Affiliations:* Phi Beta Kappa, Athenaean, and Delta Kappa Epsilon (all Bowdoin). (GCB, 56)

References: Hawthorne's original letters, held by Bowdoin, have been included in *The Letters,* multi-volume collection, ed. T. Woodson, L. N. Smith, and N. H. Pearson (Columbus, Ohio: Ohio University Press, 1984-87). To facilitate reading Hawthorne's mixed views on slavery, abolition, and blacks, start with vols. 15-18. These vols. also contain allusions to Bowdoin. See also Bridge's *Personal Recollections of Nathaniel Hawthorne* (New York: Harper & Brothers, Publishers, 1893) and his communication with Bridge regarding black soldiers fighting for their civil liberties as a prelude to their induction into American society, and as educationally laden experience.

Ezekiel Holmes (A.B. 1821, M.D. 1824) *Birth:* Aug. 24, 1801 Kingston, MA; *Death:* Feb. 9, 1867 Winthrop, ME; *Career:* Physician, Paris, Winthrop, 1832-33; Teacher, Gardiner Lyceum; Principal 1829-32; Lecturer, chemistry and natural history, Colby, 1833-37; Head, Maine State Natural Science Survey 1861-62; Editor, *Maine Farmer* 1833-65; Maine State Legislature 1836-50, 1851-52; State Senate 1844-45 (while in the Senate, he presented an amendment regarding the annexation of Texas as non-slaveholding territory); Free Soil Candidate 1852, 1853 for governor of Maine; *Professional and Social Affiliations:* member and vice president, Antislavery Society in Winthrop (1834), and wrote the society's constitution; Presiding officer, Free Soil Convention of Maine. (GCB, 439; Thurston, 103-104; Schriver, 73-75; Clark, 42).

References: Clarence L. Day, *Ezekiel Holmes: Father of Maine*

Agriculture (Orono, ME: University of Maine Press, 1968) in circulation.

General Oliver Otis Howard (A.B. 1850, A.M. 1853, Overseer 1866-74, Trustee 1892-1909, LL.D. 1888) *Birth:* Nov. 8, 1830 Leeds, ME; *Death:* October 26, 1909 Burlington, VT; *Additional Education and Honorary Degrees:* West Point 1854, LL.D. Colby 1865, LL.D. Shurtleff College 1865, LL.D. Gettysburg College 1866; LL.D. Lincoln Memorial University 1907; *Career:* Second Lieutenant, Ordnance Dept. Watervliet Arsenal, NY, and Kennebeck Arsenal, ME; Instructor of Mathematics, West Point 1857-1861; commanded and organized Third Maine Volunteers 1861; moved to Washington, D.C.; commanded brigade in first Battle of Bull Run; became Brigadier General of Volunteers 1861, commanded battles of Yorktown, Williamsburg, Fair Oaks, second battle of Bull Run, Antietam, and Fredericksburg; promoted Major General of Volunteers 1862; commanded 11th Army Corps in battles of Chancellorsville and Gettysburg; commanded the Army of Tennessee July 1864; brevetted Major General in Regular Army March 1865; made Brigadier General in Regular Army December 1865; Commissioner of the Bureau of Refugees, Freedmen and Abandoned Lands in the War Department November 1865-1871; founded Hampton Institute, Howard (President 1869-74), Atlanta, Lincoln, Fisk and Straight Universities and others, such as the Lincoln Memorial University and Industrial School for white mountain boys and girls Cumberland Gap, TN; Commander, Dept. of the Columbia 1876-80; Superintendent West Point 1881-82; *Professional and Social Affiliations:* Athenaean (Bowdoin); President, Congressional Home Missionary Society; *Family:* married Elizabeth Ann Waite Feb. 14, 1855; seven children. (GCB, 96)

References: Special Collections owns over 100,000 items in the **Oliver Otis Howard** Papers. Among the prominent figures in antislavery with whom Howard communicated were **Frederick Douglass, Sojourner Truth, Harriett Tubman, Harriet Beecher Stowe, William Wells Brown,** and **Hannibal Hamlin.** See entries under section 7. Also see Howard's letter of 1865 to Lyman Abbott re: Fiske/Knoxville and sending teachers south to teach the freedmen.

Henry Wadsworth Longfellow (A.B. 1825,[14] A.M. 1828, L.L.D. 1874; Professor of Modern Language 1829-1835; Librar-

ian 1829-1835) *Birth:* Feb. 27, 1807 Portland, ME; *Death:* March 24, 1882 Cambridge, MA; *Honorary Degrees:* L.L.D. Harvard 1859; L.L.D. Cambridge 1869; D.C.L. Oxford 1869; *Career:* Professor of French and Spanish, Harvard 1835-1854; Author, Cambridge, MA. *Professional and Social Affiliations:* Phi Beta Kappa and Peucinian Society (both Bowdoin). (GCB, 56; Cleaveland, 309)

References: Most of the known correspondence by Longfellow has been consolidated into a six-volume set, *The Letters of Henry Wadsworth Longfellow*, ed. Andrew Hilen (Cambridge: Belknap Press of Harvard University Press, 1966). Except for very recent additions, Bowdoin's letters are reprinted in that collection. See in particular vol. 1 for Longfellow's discussions of Bowdoin, and vols. 2-4 for discussions of his *Poems on Slavery*.

Joseph Cammet Lovejoy See entry under APPENDIX A.

Owen Lovejoy (1830-33, nongraduate) *Birth:* Jan. 6, 1811 Albion, ME; *Death:* March 25, 1864 Brooklyn, NY; *Career:* moved to Alton, IL 1836, Pastor, Congregational Church Princeton, IL 1839-56; member of U.S. Congress 1856-1864 (Republican); *Professional and Social Affiliations:* active in the Illinois abolitionist movement 1835-60s, Peucinian Society (Bowdoin). (BDC, 1478)

References: Alumni Pamphlets: (speeches delivered in the House of Representatives): *The Fanaticism of the Democratic Party*, February 21, 1859; *Conduct of War*, January 6, 1862; *Confiscation of Rebel Property,. . . Reply to Messrs Crittenden and Wickliffe of Kentucky. . .* , April 24, 1862.

Alpheus Spring Packard (A.B. 1816, A.M. 1819, D.D. 1860; Professor of Language and Classic Literature 1816-1819; Tutor of Language and Mathematics 1819-1822; Professor of Language and Metaphysics 1822-24; Professor of Language and Classical Literature 1824-1842; Rhetoric, Oratory, Classical Literature 1842-1845; Ancient Language, Classical Literature 1845-1865; Collins Professor 1864-1884; Librarian 1869-1881; Acting President 1883-1884) *Birth:* December 23, 1798 Chelmsford, MA; *Death:* July 13, 1884 Squirrel Island, ME; *Career:* edited *History of Bowdoin College*. Packard taught and served in official capacities at Bowdoin College from graduation to his death in 1884. **William Smyth** and Packard shared a duplex for nearly 45 years. *Professional and Social Affiliations:* Peucinian Society and Phi Beta Kappa (both Bowdoin). (GCB, 49)

Reference: Correspondence: Sept. 14, 1846, records Packard's response to the Queen of England's statement of July 15, 1852. In this letter he mentions an agent of the Antislavery Society, S. L. Wilson, on the Gabon River.

Albion Keith Parris See entry under APPENDIX A.

Swan L. Pomeroy See entry under BOWDOIN OVERSEERS, TRUSTEES, AND PRESIDENTS.

George Lewis Prentiss (A.B. 1835, A.M. 1838, D.D. 1854) *Birth:* May 12, 1816 Gorham, ME; *Death:* March 18, 1903 New York; *Additional Education:* Studied in Halle and Berlin, Germany 1839-41; *Career:* Clergy, New Bedford, MA 1845-50, New York 1851-58, 1862-73; Professor, pastoral theology, Union Theological Seminary 1873-1903; *Professional and Social Affiliations:* Phi Beta Kappa and Peucinian (both Bowdoin). (GCB, 70)

References: Alumni Pamphlets: *The Free Christian State and the Present Struggle. An Address Delivered Before the Association of the Alumni of Bowdoin College* (New York: John A. Gray, printer, stereotyper and binder, 1861), which mentions "wholesale prosecution of the African slave trade, under the protection of the American flag; fillibusterism, Floydism, and the new gospel of the divine institution, beneficience, and unlimited extension of Negro slavery" (23), as well as the use of the "state's rights" argument as an excuse to avoid agitation; *The Political Situation* (New York, 1866) contains a discussion of "Religious Sentiment of the North" regarding their duty to the Freedmen, Lincoln and Reconstruction, Negro Suffrage, and the Radical Abolitionists.

John Brown Russwurm (A.B. 1826, Medical School 1826, A.M. 1829) *Birth:* Oct. 1, 1799 Port Antonio, Jamaica; *Death:* June 17, 1851 Cape Palmas, Africa; *Education:* 1819 Hebron Academy; *Career:* Teacher, Boston, MA 1819; Co-founder and editor *Freedom's Journal* 1827-1829, first black newspaper in the U.S.; Superintendent of Schools in Liberia 1829; Publisher and editor of *Liberia Herald* 1830-35; Colonial secretary in Liberia 1830-34; Governor of Cape Palmas (also referred to as Governor of Maryland, Liberia, Africa) 1836-51; *Family:* married Sarah McGill 1835, 3 sons, 1 daughter; *Professional and Social Affiliations:* Athenaean Society (Bowdoin). (GCB, 58; DANB, 538-39)[15]

References: 1826 Commencement part, "The Conditions and

Prospects of Hayti"; an acceptance to the Athenaean Society; votes of the Governing Boards of Bowdoin College to grant degrees to Russwurm; brief biography; letter from James Hall to A. Cleaveland containing biographical information on Russwurm; Rowland Bailey Howard Papers, letter from Russwurm to John Otis, North Yarmouth, June 22, 1819; copies of Russwurm letters to half-brother Francis Edward Russwurm and cousin John S. Russwurm from the Manuscript Section of the Tennessee State Library and Archives, Nashville, TN; article on Russwurm in *Down East: The Magazine of Maine*, June 1972; numerous biographical newspaper clippings, as well as facsimiles of partial issues of *Freedom's Journal*; Mary Sagarin's *John Brown Russwurm: The Story of "Freedom's Journal," Freedom's Journey* (New York: Lothrop, Lee & Shepard, 1970), an out-of-print biography; Sagarin's text contains the program of a 1952 meeting commemorating the 125th anniversary of the Black press. The cover is a reproduction of the first issue of *Freedom's Journal* with a superimposed picture of Russwurm.

George Shepard (D.D. 1846) *Birth:* Aug. 26, 1801 Plainfield, CT; *Death:* March 23, 1868; Sought the faith through Orin Fowler, Amherst, MA; *Education:* A.B. Amherst College 1824, Andover Theological Seminary 1827; *Career:* Pastor, First Congregational Church of Hallowell, ME, or Old South Church, Feb. 1828-36 (succeeded **Rev. Elipalet Gillet**, pastor from 1795 to 1827); Professor of Homilectics, Bangor Theological Seminary 1836-68; *Professional and Social Affiliations:* Phi Beta Kappa (Amherst); Corresponding secretary of the first Maine Anti-Slavery Society; *Family:* married Lydia Fuller of Plainfield, CT, eight children, four girls and four boys; son **George Henry Shepard** 1855. (GCB, 548; Clark, 66)

References: Alumni Pamphlets: *The Duty of Helping the Weak*, A Sermon delivered in Bangor, June 24, 1835, before the Maine Missionary Society; also *Discourse Commemorative of Benjamin Tappan*; Dole papers, Letter to **Ebenezer Dole**, May 13, 1834. See also *Letters of William Lloyd Garrison*, ed. Walter M. Merrill, vol. 1 (Cambridge, MA: Harvard University Press, 1971).

Egbert C. Smyth (A.B. 1848, D.D. 1866, LL.D. 1902, Tutor in Greek 1849-51, Professor of Rhetoric and Oratory 1854-56, Collins Professor of Natural and Revealed Religion 1856-63,

Overseer 1874-77, Trustee 1877-1904) *Birth:* Aug. 24, 1829 Brunswick, ME; *Death:* April 12, 1904 Andover, MA; *Additional Education and Honorary Degree:* Bangor Theological Seminary 1853; D.D. Harvard 1886; *Career:* Teacher, Farmington, NH; Clergy (ordained Congregational Ministry 1856); Professor, ecclesiastical history, Andover Theological Seminary 1863-1904; *Family:* son of **William Smyth**; nephew of Egbert Benson Coffin A.B. 1823; married Elizabeth B. Dwight (daughter of **William Theodore Dwight**); *Professional and Social Affiliations:* member, American Antiquarian Society, American Historical Assoc., New England Historic Genealogical Society, Massachusetts Historical Society, Prudential Committee of the American Board (1875-86). (GCB, 93)[16]

References: Alumni Pamphlets: "Our Country Not Forsaken of God: A Sermon Preached to the Students of Bowdoin College, in the Congregational Church, Brunswick, June 23, 1861," in which he urges students to join the cause to abolish slavery in the name of Christianity.

William Smyth (A.B. 1822; A.M. 1825; D.D. 1863; Asst. Professor of Mathematics and Natural Philosophy 1825-28; Professor of Mathematics 1828-68; Associate Professor of Natural Philosophy 1846-59, Professor 1859-68) *Birth:* Feb. 1, 1797 Pittston, ME; *Death:* April 4, 1868 Brunswick, ME; *Additional Education and Honorary Degrees:* Andover Theological Seminary 1822-23; LL. D. Illinois College 1866; *Career:* Assistant Principal, Gorham Academy 1817-1820; served in the War of 1812; Tutor, Greek 1823-25; Editor, *Advocate of Freedom,* Brunswick, ME 1838); *Family:* married Harriet Coffin in 1827; seven children, among whom four sons attended Bowdoin: **Egbert Coffin Smyth** (see entry above), **Edward Beecher Smyth** (1850-51), **William Henry Smyth** (A.B. 1856), and **George Adams Smyth** (A.B. 1868, A.M. 1871, Med. School 1869-70); *Professional and Social Affiliations:* Peucinian Society and Phi Beta Kappa (both Bowdoin); Vice President of General Alumni Association 1861-1868; member First Congregational Church of Brunswick, ME; Corresponding secretary, Maine Anti-Slavery Society (prepared annual report of the society's activities); with **David Thurston** and **Silas McKeen**, he organized the only known Congregational Antislavery Society meeting, held on June 25, 1839, in Brunswick. (GCB, 53; Willey, 120, 123, 156; Schriver, 28, 89n; Cleaveland, 247-48).

References: numerous contributions to *Advocate of Freedom*, especially during period he served as editor (March 8, 1838-April 25, 1839); Biographical File: 12 manuscripts and 7 newspaper clippings; "An Inquisition of 1835" in Minot and Snow, *Tales of Bowdoin* (Augusta: Press of the Kennebec Journal, 1901); also check Abbott Memorial Collection: Lyman Abbott-Cyrus Hamlin Correspondence, letter of Smyth to Hamlin, March 6, 1843, in which Smyth comments on the present state of the antislavery movement, in particular, the conflict between the mass of abolitionists and the Garrisonians; see also the Alumni Biographical Files under Robert Hallowell Gardiner.

Thomas Treadwell Stone (A.B. 1820, A.M. 1823, D.D. 1868)
Birth: Feb. 9, 1801 Waterford, ME; *Death:* Nov. 13, 1895; *Additional Education:* attended Hebron College before Bowdoin; studied theology in Augusta; *Career:* Clergy (ordained a Congregationalist in 1824 but changed to Unitarianism by 1846), Andover 1824-30, First Congregational East Machias 1832-46, First Church of Salem, MA 1846-52, Bolton, MA 1842-60, Brooklyn, CT 1863-71; Principal, Bridgton Academy 1830-32; Lecturer, Lowell Institute 1858; *Professional and Social Affiliations:* Phi Beta Kappa and Athenaean (Bowdoin); a transcendentalist; signed list calling for an antislavery convention in Augusta, 1834; corresponding secretary of the Anti-Slavery Society formed in East Machias in 1838. (GCB, 51; Clark, 43, 82)

References: Alumni Pamphlets: *The Martyr of Freedom, A Discourse delivered at East Machias Nov. 30 and Dec. 7, 1837* (Boston: Isaac Knapp, 1838), is a tribute to Elijah P. Lovejoy, but is also critical of those who fail to oppose slavery vocally; *An Address Before the Salem Female Anti-Slavery Society at its Annual Meeting, Dec. 7, 1851* (Salem, 1852) re: "The Anti-Slavery movement proposes merely the Divine Law of Justice and Love as the principle by which all our intercourse with those now held in slavery shall be regulated" (13). In Biographical File: obituary, Boston Journal, Nov. 15, 1895, states that Stone was forced to leave his pulpit in Salem because he freely expressed his abolitionist views; newspaper clipping, *The Christian Register*, Nov. 28, 1895, labels Stone "an uncompromising abolitionist." See bibliography, *Stone's Private Library*, which contains works by such antislavers as Lydia Maria Child, Channing, and Theodore Parker. Also see his articles in the *Liberty Standard* and the *Christian Mirror*.

Calvin Ellis Stowe See entry under APPENDIX A.

John Searle Tenney (A.B. 1816, A.M. 1819, LL.D. 1850, Overseer 1842-49, Trustee 1849-69; Lecturer to Professor of Medical Jurisprudence 1849-69) *Birth:* Jan. 21, 1793 Rowley, MA; *Death:* Aug. 23, 1869 Norridgewock, ME; *Career:* Lawyer, Norridgewock; Maine Legislature 1838; Maine Senate 1864-65; Justice, Maine Supreme Judicial Court 1841-55, Chief Justice, Maine Supreme Judicial Court 1855-62; *Professional and Social Affiliations:* Phi Beta Kappa, Peucinian Society, Delta Kappa Epsilon (all Bowdoin). (GCB, 49)

References: Biographical File: See "Opinions of Judges Tenney and Cutting" in *Opinions of the Several Justices of the S. J. Court, on the Constitutionality of Personal Liberty Laws of the State of Maine* (Augusta: Stevens & Sayward, 1861) (5-7), re: Tenney reasons that Maine's Personal Liberty Laws are not in conflict with the 1850 Fugitive Slave Law; occasional letters printed in *Advocate of Freedom* (letter of July 4, 1839, makes reference to "the philanthropic enterprise, which abolitionists are prosecuting").

Richard Hampton Vose (A.B. 1822, A.M. 1825, Overseer 1841-1864) *Birth:* Nov. 8, 1803 Northfield, MA; *Death:* Jan. 19, 1864 Augusta, ME; *Additional Education:* studied law for three years; *Career:* worked in Gov. Lincoln's office; Lawyer, Worcester, MA 1826-28, Augusta, ME 1828-64; Maine Legislature 1834-35, 1838-39; State Senate 1840-41; Pres. 1841; prosecuting officer for Kennebec; *Professional and Social Affiliations:* Phi Beta Kappa and Peucinian Society (both Bowdoin); member of committee of the Augusta Anti-Slavery Society to draft resolutions and constitution, 1838. (GCB, 53)[17]

References: One item "A Poem Delivered on the Anniversary of the Literary Fraternity of Waterville [now Colby] College, July 26, 1831," which lyricizes that the institution of slavery brings "shame to the land, whose motto ought to be, All men are equal, by their nature free—."

NOTES

[1] Appleton argued that of the Supreme Court's nine separate opinions only three specifically denied black citizenship. Moreover, that nowhere in the Constitution is it expressed or implied that "free men of African descent are prohibited from becoming citizens of a state . . . and as such . . . citizens of the United States." Appleton proved Taney wrong by stating that "the necessary degradation of the slave affords no reason for the denial of citizenship to the free man." Appleton cited the fact that blacks had fought in the Revolutionary Army, expressed their vows of allegiance, owned real estate, and were and continued to be acknowledged as citizens in several states. "If these things be so," he continued, "and that they are so cannot be denied or even doubted, and if they had been known to the learned Chief Justice, his conclusions would have been different." (19-32).

[2] James M. McPherson, "Coercion or Conciliation? Abolitionists Debate President Hayes's Southern Policy," *New England Quarterly* 39 (1966): 483-84.

[3] Brigadier General Henry Goddard Thomas (1837 Portland—1897) was commissioned first colonel of the 79th U.S. Colored Infantry and, on Jan. 16, 1864, of the 19th Colored Infantry. He is considered the first officer of the Regular Army to have accepted a colonelcy of "colored" troops. He was appointed to Ferrero's IX Corps division of "colored" troops at the beginning of U. S. Grant's Overland Campaign and was involved in all the battles thereafter, including the Battle of the Carter (*Generals in Blue*, 502).

[4] For more information on Blaine, see David Saville Muzzey, *James G. Blaine: A Political Idol of Other Days* (New York: Dodd, Mead and Company, 1934).

[5] **Bradbury** is not fully entered in this guide because of his pro-South leanings and advocacy of the private property rights of slaveholders. See "Letter from Hon. James W. Bradbury" in *Bangor Daily Union Report of the Grand Union Meeting*...(1860).

[6] **Franklin Pierce A.B. 1824, LL.D 1854** is not an appropriate subject for this guide because of his pro-property rights stance, antagonism for anti-slavery agitation, and for sectional animosities. See *Papers of Franklin Pierce, 1820-1869* (Washington: Library of Congress, 1959).

[7] **William Lloyd Garrison** was associated with **George** and **Henry Cheever**, as is evident by allusions to them in his letters and other autobiographical materials. For example, see Wendell Phillips Garrison, *William Lloyd Garrison, 1805-1879, The Story of His Life Told by His Children* 4 vols. New York: The Century Co., 1885-89. See also Lawrence J. Friedman, *Gregarious Saints: Self and Community in American Abolitionism, 1830-1870* (Cambridge: Cambridge University Press, 1982), passim, for numerous references to the Cheever brothers.

[8] One copy is autographed "For the Peucinian Society of Bowdoin

College Presented by the Author, New York Dec. 22, 1862." Handwritten in a second copy is "Presented by **Henry Cheever**."

[9] This letter is probably associated with the case of James Sagurs, who charged Daniel Philbrook, master of the Schooner or Brig *Susan,* and Edward Kelleran, mate of the vessel, with facilitating the freedom of his slave Atticus. Much correspondence was exchanged from 1837 to 1839 between the governors of Maine and Georgia. The governors of Georgia (William Schley and George Gilmer) demanded the extradition of the fugitive, but the governors of Maine (including Robert Dunlap, Edward Kent, and Fairfield) refused to cooperate with the slave laws. The bulk of this correspondence is in the Maine State Archives.

[10] Copy is autographed, "To My Kinsman, Timothy C. Fessenden from the Author. Sept. 9, 1875, Stamford, CT."

[11] In 1854, he was elected by Free Soil Democrats.

[12] George Henry Preble, *William Pitt Fessenden: A Memoir* (Prepared for the New England Historical and Genealogical Register for April 1871) (Boston: David Clapp & Son, Printers, 1871); Francis Fessenden, *Life and Public Service of William Pitt Fessenden.* 2 vols. (Boston: Houghton, Mifflin & Co., 1907); see also in the Biographical File: William Salter, *William Pitt Fessenden* (Des Moines, Iowa: Historical Dept., 1908).

[13] Penelope Campbell makes extensive references to **Hall** in *Maryland in Africa: The Maryland State Colonization Society 1831-1857* (Univ. of Illinois Press, 1971).

[14] **Longfellow** entered Bowdoin at the age of fourteen with his fifteen-year-old brother, **Stephen,** but felt so out of place that, although he was technically in residence, he spent much of his time at home in Portland, Maine.

[15] The following biography is also available at the Russwurm Africana Center Library at Bowdoin: Janice Borzendowski, *John Russwurm,* ed. Nathan I. Huggins (New York: Chelsea House Publishers, 1989). See also Campbell, passim.

[16] For additional biographical and interpretative notes, see Edward Stanwood, *Memoir of Egbert Coffin Smyth* (Boston: Massachusetts Historical Society, 1910); and Edward Young Hicks, *Memoir of Egbert Coffin Smyth* (Boston: David Clapp & Son, 1904).

[17] See *Record of the Augusta Anti-Slavery Society* (1838).

Winslow Homer (American, 1836-1910). Expulsion of the Negroes and Abolitionists from Tremont Temple, Boston, on December 3, 1860, *wood engraving. Bowdoin College Museum of Art, Brunswick, Maine. 1974.1.55. Originally published in Harper's Weekly, December 15, 1860.*

3
Bowdoin Student Organizations

The Peucinian and Athenaean Societies were rival literary organizations in the nineteenth century at Bowdoin. Although interest in the societies died out by the early 1870s, their extensive libraries remained and were greatly needed by the college community. When they flourished, these groups were significantly different—socially, economically, and politically, especially in the 1820s. The Peucinian and Athenaean societies "typified respectively"—as Hawthorne in his *Letters* later described them—"the respectable conservative and the progressive or democratic parties." The Peucinians were likely to be Whigs; the Athenaeans, Democrats. In the presidential election of 1824 the Peucinians inclined to John Quincy Adams; the Athenaeans to Andrew Jackson. Randall Steward, a biographer of Hawthorne, has said that the Peucinians were "the best students" and the Athenaeans were "jolly good fellows." See *Nathaniel Hawthorne: A Biography* (New Haven: Yale, 1948), passim.

The library catalogs of these societies indicate interest in antislavery in America and Britain as early as the 1820s. The *Catalogue of the Library of the Peucinian Society* for 1829 contains works by the prominent British abolitionist William Wilberforce, and the catalog for 1834 lists Thomas Clarkson's systematic argument against the slave trade, *On the Slavery and Commerce of the Human Species*, and William Lloyd Garrison's denunciation of colonization, *Thoughts on African Colonization*, as well as contemporary periodicals promoting the Colonizationist proposition. Clearly competitive with this collection was the *Catalogue of the Athenaean Society Library* of 1838, which also included works by Wilberforce, as well as A. A. Phelps's *Lectures on Slavery, Memoirs of E. P. Lovejoy* (by his brothers Joseph and Owen), and Mrs. Lydia Childs's *A Plea for Slaves* and *The Rebels: A Novel*.

The libraries were often enriched by gifts made in memory of a deceased member. Footnoted throughout this book, especially in APPENDIX B, for instance, are volumes given in memory of **Rev. Henry Cheever** or one of the **Fessendens**. These volumes are especially valuable and symbolic as they perpetuate in substance the principle of emancipation, about which those for whom they were given so tirelessly preached and legislated.

ATHENAEAN SOCIETY

Founded in 1808, said to have been founded by a former "disgruntled" member of the Peucinian Society who did not graduate (name not mentioned); first society to found a library; obtained a charter of incorporation from the Bowdoin legislature in 1828; admitted freshmen, unlike the Peucinian Society; officers were president, vice-president, orator at anniversaries & poets.

Prominent members: John Albion Andrew, John P. Hale, James Hall, William Pitt Fessenden, Nathaniel Hawthorne, John Brown Russwurm, Thomas Treadwell Stone.

PEUCINIAN SOCIETY

Organized November 22, 1805; name changed from the Philomathian Society to the Peucinian Society; did not admit freshmen; established a library with approximately 7,000 volumes; obtained a charter in 1833; officers were president, vice-president, orators at anniversaries & poets. Calvin Ellis Stowe Papers contain Peucinian *Society Records,* vol. 3, 1819-1831, which include minutes by Stowe, who was society secretary in 1822-23.

Prominent members: John Appleton, George Barrell Cheever, Henry T. Cheever, Edward Francis Cutter, William Cutter, Philip Eastman, Joseph Palmer Fessenden, Charles Freeman, William Pierce Frye, Henry Wadsworth Longfellow, Joseph C. Lovejoy, Owen Lovejoy, Alpheus Spring Packard, George L. Prentiss, John Searle Tenney, Calvin Ellis Stowe, William Smyth, Richard Hampton Vose.

4
Bowdoin Overseers, Trustees, and Presidents

Aaron Chester Adams See entry under BOWDOIN ALUMNI.

George Eliashib Adams See entry under APPENDIX A.

John Appleton See entry under BOWDOIN ALUMNI.

John White Chickering See entry under APPENDIX A.

Asa Cummings (Overseer 1821-49, Trustee 1849-56, A.M. 1825, D.D. 1847) *Birth:* Sept. 29, 1790 Andover, MA; Death: June 5, 1856, at sea; *Education:* A.B. Harvard 1817, A.M. Harvard 1820; studied at Andover Theological Seminary 1820; *Career:* Tutor at Andover, MA in math and metaphysics 1819-20; Clergy, North Yarmouth, ME, 1821-29: Editor, *Christian Mirror* (Portland, ME) 1826-55[1]; *Professional and Social Affiliations:* member, Auxiliary Colonization Society of Maine; member, Board of Trustees, Maine Missionary Board, 1825-48; Member, Maine Congregational Conference, 1838. (GCB, 7; Willey, 118; Schriver, 4, 17; Clark, 20, 58)

References: Alumni Pamphlets: *Discourse delivered at Brunswick, ME, April 6, 1820, the Day of the Annual Fast in Maine and Massachusetts,* in which he stated: "This outrage upon justice and humanity. This traffick in human flesh, this oppression of the poor and friendless, will certainly sink the nation that authorizes it, unless their doom be averted by speedy repentance; unless they 'undo the heavy burdens and let the oppressed go free and break every yoke'" (24). Though Cummings was against slavery, he was at odds with abolitionists, as the following quote from the Biographical File reveals: "this is the time to say—that on nearly every point in which Father Cummings was at issue with the abolitionists twenty years ago, the public sentiment of the North has decided in his favor. One point at issue was with reference to the expediency of immediate and universal emancipation. Another point was as to whether the mere relation of master and slave was necessarily a sin per se. Another point had reference to the extent of our civil responsibility for the removal of slavery from the Southern States"; see "The New Years Address" in *The Christian Mirror*, Dec. 27, 1859.

Edward Francis Cutter See entry under BOWDOIN ALUMNI.

William Cutter See entry under APPENDIX A.

Woodbury Davis (Overseer 1865-67) *Birth:* July 26, 1818 Portland, ME; *Death:* August 13, 1871; *Career:* Lawyer, Portland, ME; Judge, Maine Supreme Court, 1855-56, 1857-65; *Professional and Social Affiliations:* staff of Liberty Party, and chosen as delegate to Maine Liberty Association; secretary, State Religious Antislavery Convention; deeply religious; member of the newly formed Maine Colonization Society, 1855.[2] (GCB, 8; Schriver, 59, 74n, 104n-105n)

References: Biographical File: newspaper article, "Impeachment of Judge Woodbury Davis," *Lewiston Journal* June 8-11, 1910; see "Opinion of Judge Davis" in *Opinions of the Several Justices of the S. J. Sourt, on the Constitutionality of the Personal Liberty Laws of the State of Maine* (Augusta: Stevens & Sayward, 1861), in which he claimed that the Fugitive Slave Law violated the Constitution in several instances: it called for a summary extradition hearing; it allowed the prisoner, instead of receiving a trial, to be released to a private party, who could re-sell him into slavery. Davis felt that the latter action constituted a violation of the person's right to liberty and that the fugitive slave tribunal as final and unappealable was in violation of the constitutional guarantee of habeas corpus. He concluded tht the Personal Liberty Laws of Maine were not in "contravention of any law of the United States" (41-47).[3]

William Theodore Dwight (Overseer 1839-60) *Birth:* June 15, 1795 Greenfield, CT; *Death:* Oct. 22, 1865 Andover, MA; *Education:* A.B. Yale 1813, A.M. Yale 1816, D.D. Bowdoin 1846; *Career:* Tutor, Yale 1817-19; Lawyer, Philadelphia, PA 1821-31; Clergy (ordained June 6, 1832) Portland, ME, Third Parish (Congregational); Second Parish of Portland 1832-64; *Professional and Social Affiliations:* Phi Beta Kappa (Bowdoin); Member, Maine Congregational Conference; one of seventeen signers to form a new Maine Colonization Society (1854); *Family:* son of President

Timothy Dwight of Yale. (GCB, 8; Willey, 118; Clark, 90, 176)[4]
References: Biographical Files (Bowdoin Boards): two letters to Nathan Dole (Portland, Sept. 28, 1848; Portland, April 25, 1849) re: Review of the *Report by the Synod of West Tennessee on the Subject of Slavery*; second letter, Dwight renders a detailed summary of the report, which mildly condemns slavery and apologizes for Southern Congregationalists' commitment to the institution.

Philip Eastman See entry under APPENDIX A.

John Wallace Ellingwood See entry under APPENDIX A.

Samuel Fessenden (Overseer 1822-29, LL.D. 1846) *Birth:* July 16, 1784 Fryeburg, ME; *Death:* March 19, 1869 Portland, ME; *Education and Honorary Degrees:* A.B. Dartmouth 1806; studied law under Hon. Judah Dana of Fryeburg; *Career:* Teacher, Fryeburg (before college); Teacher, Paris, ME, and Boscawen, NH (during college); Lawyer (admitted to the Bar in 1809) and politician, started in New Gloucester; Massachusetts State Legislature 1814, 1815, 1816, 1825, and 1826; Massachusetts State Senate (Cumberland County) 1818, 1819; Major General of the 10th Division of the Militia of Massachusetts 1818; Major General of the Twelfth Division of Massachusetts 1819-33; 1822 moved to Portland, ME, law partnership with Thomas Avory Dublois until 1854; private practice with his son, Daniel W. Fessenden 1854-61; *Professional and Social Affiliations:* Phi Beta Kappa (Dartmouth); member, Maine Historical Society; abandoned colonizationism after hearing **Garrison** in 1833; was principal in establishing the Portland Anti-Slavery Society and the Ladies Anti-Slavery Sewing Society in 1833; co-founder (Oct. 15, 1834) and regularly elected president of the Maine Anti-Slavery Society; ran for governor on the Liberty Party ticket 1841, and from 1845 to 1848; helped organize the Free Soil Party in 1848; represented the Free Soil Party in gubernatorial races 1848-53; President, Free Democratic Association (organized by Portland Free Soilers)[5]; received the first antislavery Congressional nomination for the Portland area in 1842; remained an ardent abolitionist and leader of the Maine Anti-Slavery Society his entire life[6]; *Family:* married Deborah Chandler Dec. 16, 1813; eleven children, and an illegitimate son, **William Pitt Fessenden**. (GCB, 9; Schriver, 5-9, 14, 21-23, 56-58, 63, 66-67, 74-76)[7]

References: See APPENDIX D. The Fessenden Papers (120 letters) contains correspondence from a roll-call of notable figures in antislavery: William Lord Blair, John Curtis Caldwell, William Allen, Salmon P. Chase, Frederick Douglass, Neal Dow, Nelson Dingley, Jr., William Lloyd Garrison, Hannibal Hamlin, Abraham Lincoln, Wendell Phillips, Carl Schurz, William Henry Seward, Lyman Trumbull, Israel Washburn, Jr., and Jabez Howard Woodman, to name a few.

William Pitt Fessenden See entry under BOWDOIN ALUMNI.

Charles Freeman See entry under BOWDOIN ALUMNI.

William Pierce Frye See entry under BOWDOIN ALUMNI.

Robert Hallowell Gardiner See entry under APPENDIX A.

Dr. Eliphalet Gillet (Overseer 1798-1816, Trustee 1816-1848) *Birth:* Nov. 19, 1768 Colchester, CT; *Death:* Oct. 19, 1848; *Education:* A.B. Dartmouth 1791, A.M. Dartmouth 1794, D.D. University of Vermont 1824; *Career:* Pastor, First Congregational Church of Hallowell 1795-1828; *Family:* married 1805 Mary Gurley; eleven children; *Professional and Social Affiliations:* Phi Beta Kappa (Dartmouth); one of the early supporters of the Colonization Society (brother-in-law of Ralph Gurley, a leading officer of the Colonization Society); Secretary, Maine Missionary Society (at his Hallowell residence in 1807) 1807-48, and was paid $8.00 per week plus other expenses as the society's regional agent. (GCB, 10; Schriver, 4)[8]

References: Biographical File: newspaper clipping, "Centennial of Maine Missionary Society," *Lewiston Weekly Journal*, May 8, 1907; *Thanksgiving: A Discourse Delivered at Hallowell on the Day of the Annual Thanksgiving in Massachusetts, December 2, 1819* (Hallowell, ME: E. Goodale, 1819) alludes to the "poor African, whose birthright has been ignorance, time immemorial"; *Evils of Intemperance: A Sermon Preached at Hallowell, on the Day of the Annual Fast in Maine, April 12, 1821* (Hallowell, ME: Goodale, Glazier & Co., 1821) in which he comments: "Men loudly complain, and with great justice, at the extension of slavery. It is an evil not to be endured. Vengeance is supposed to be in reserve for those who inflict it. It takes from a man his birthright;

the privileges granted him, as by a charter from heaven" (13). However, Gillet perceives intemperance a greater evil than human enslavement.

John Holmes (Trustee 1821-43) *Birth:* March 28,1773 Kingston, MA; *Death:* July 7, 1843 Portland, ME; *Education:* A.B. Brown 1796, M.A. Brown 1799; *Career:* Lawyer, Alfred, ME; MA Legislature, 1802-03, 1812; MA Senate, 1813-16; Congress, 1817-20; ME Constitutional Convention, 1819; ME Legislature, 1829, 1835-37; U. S. Senate 1820-27, 1829-33; *Family:* both sons attended Bowdoin: William Bradford 1823, Charles Henry nongraduate 1829. (GCB, 10; Willey, 42)

References: Alumni Pamphlets: three speeches—*Delivered in the Senate of the U.S. February 18, 1830 on the debate which arose upon Mr. Foote's Resolution Relative to Public Lands* (Cooper 1897), see for a discussion of his equivocal views on slavery; *Oration delivered at Alfred on July 4, 1815* (American Imprints, S&S 34942); and *Speech of. . . on the Annual Appropriation Bill against the Policy of the Administration in Regard to Diplomatic Intercourse, the Colonial Trade, and Northeastern Boundary Delivered in the Senate of the U.S., April 9, 10, 11, 1832.* Inconspicuously subsumed in the latter are his views about the African slave trade. Holmes is cited by Willey as catering to the "slave power" in order to achieve Maine's statehood, but actually Holmes waffled on the slavery issue (42), as the Alumni Pamphlets show.

William Ladd (Overseer 1825-40) *Birth:* May 10, 1778 Exeter, NH; *Death:* April 9, 1841 Portsmouth, NH; *Education:* A.B. Harvard 1797; *Career:* Merchant, Portsmouth, NH; *Professional and Social Affiliations:* President, Maine Union in Behalf of the Colored Race (lived in Minot, ME); President, American Peace Society (founded the society in 1828); representative from Maine at the organization of the American Union for the Relief and Improvement of the Colored Race (1835); *Family:* married Sophia Ann Stidolph of London. (GCB, 11; Clark, 57, 114)[9]

References: Biographical File: article about him in the *Boston Herald*, Feb. 21, 1954, stated: "He followed the sea until 1800, lived a few months in Savannah, Georgia as a merchant; then to Florida on a Cotton Plantation, where he undertook the abolition of slavery by introducing free labor in persons of European Dutch emigrants"; Alumni Pamphlets: *Address delivered at Portland, February 6, 1824 before the Peace Society of Maine* (Port-

Law of the Constitution of the United States. Also contended that an individual's national citizenship derived from state citizenship, and state citizenship determined one's right to vote (8-18).

Egbert C. Smyth See entry under BOWDOIN ALUMNI.

Benjamin Tappan See entry under APPENDIX A.

John Searle Tenney See entry under BOWDOIN ALUMNI.

David Thurston (Overseer 1832-64) *Birth:* Feb. 6, 1779 Georgetown, MA; *Death:* May 7, 1865 Litchfield, ME; *Education:* A.B. Dartmouth 1804, A.M. Dartmouth 1807, studied theology with Dr. Burton of Thetford, VT, D.D. Dartmouth 1853; *Career:* Clergy (preached first sermon at Oxford, NH on July 4, 1805), Congregational Church of Winthrop, ME 1807-51, Vassalborough 1852-54, Searsport 1855-57, Litchfield 1859-65; *Professional and Social Affiliations:* Phi Beta Kappa (Dartmouth), President, American Missionary Association; President, Maine branch of the American Education Society; committed himself to antislavery in 1820s; delegate in December 1833 to the founding convention of the American Anti-Slavery Society, member of the committee that drafted the Declaration of Sentiments and one of its first signers; cofounder with **Samuel Fessenden** of the Maine Anti-Slavery Society; Agent, American Anti-Slavery Society 1837-38; attended International Antislavery Convention in Scotland; President, Winthrop Antislavery Society (founded March 4, 1834).[10] (Willey, 116-17; GCB, 16; Thurston, 154; Schriver, 23-29; Clark, passim)

References: Various newspaper clippings from the *Advocate of Freedom* (e.g. "Appeal to Congregational Ministers in Maine, who are not members of the Anti-Slavery Society," June 7, 1838); *Causes of an unsuccessful ministry. A sermon at the ordination of the Rev. Samuel Johnson*, Hallowell, ME, 1819; *Sermon at the ordination of the Rev. David Starret*, Hallowell, ME, 1821; *A Sermon preached, May 10, 1826, at the ordination of the Rev. Josiah Tucker over the Congregational Church and Society in Madison. . .* , Hallowell, ME, 1826; *A Sermon delivered in Saco, June 26, 1816, before the Maine Missionary Society, at their ninth annual meeting*, Hallowell, ME; *A Sermon delivered at Winthrop, April 7, 1825, the annual fast in Maine*, Augusta, ME, 1825; *A Sermon preached at the ordination of Rev.*

David Smith..., Hallowell, ME, 1811. References to his antislavery activities appear in *Maine Historical Quarterly* 22 (Summer 1982): 64-79; Foster's *History of Winthrop, 1771-1971*, and *A Sketch in the Life of David Thurston*, by Thomas Adams, all at the Maine Historical Society, Portland, ME.

Leonard Woods (President 1839-66) *Birth:* Nov. 24, 1807 Newbury, MA (now West Newbury); *Death:* Dec. 24, 1878, Boston, MA; *Education:* Phillips Academy, Hanover, NH; A.B. Union College 1827; A.M. Union; D.D. Colby 1839; D.D. Harvard 1846; Student, Andover Theological Seminary 1830; *Career:* Instructor, Andover 1830-32; published edition of *Knapps Theology*, 1834-39: editor of *Literary and Theological Review* in New York, 1836-39; Professor of Biblical Literature, Bangor Theological Seminary 1836-39; *Professional and Social Affiliations:* Phi Beta Kappa (Union); one of the vice presidents of the newly formed Maine Colonization Society, 1855. *Family:* never married.[11] (GCB, 3; Clark, 175-76)

Reference: Biographical File: letter dated June 1841, Paris, to Robert Hallowell Gardner, in which he comments: "[Mr. Wayland] we encountered very harshly by the Anti-slavery spirit in England, wh. [which] is particularly rampant in the dissenting connexcions [*sic*]. From the Baptist point of view, of course everything in this old Christiandom [*sic*] must look awry."

Richard Hampton Vose See entry under BOWDOIN ALUMNI.

NOTES

[1] *Christian Mirror* (Congregational Church weekly) adopted gradualism rather than immediate emancipation, and advocated colonization (Schriver 114-15).
[2] Maine Colonization Society (1855) had as its object "to advance the cause of freedom, and to promote the elevation and civilization of the African race."
[3] **Davis** argued that the Constitution was an antislavery document incorporating the natural-rights ideals of the Declaration of Independence. He concurred with the interpretation of the Constitution phrased by **Salmon P. Chase** and the Liberty Party men of the 1830s and 1840s that focused on the Declaration as the crucial point from which to start. Davis continued that the framers of the Constitution had deliberately

avoided the use of the terms "slavery," and "servitude"; instead, they used the word "service," which evidenced that slavery could eventually be abolished without amending the Constitution.

[4] See *A Sketch of the Life and Ministry of William T. Dwight; with an Appendix* (Boston: Nichols, and Noyes, 1869) by his son-in-law **Egbert C. Smyth**. This Alumni Pamphlet of Smyth's contains a list of Dwight's publications.

[5] According to Schriver, this society focused on antislavery and temperance.

[6] **Fessenden** is credited with introducing Macon B. Allen (an African American) into the Maine District Court in 1814 while the court was in session, and he moved that Allen be granted permission to practice law in the state of Maine.

[7] See the unpublished "Account of Gen. Samuel Fessenden and Family" by grandson Francis Fessenden, which states that Samuel was an immediatist, supported the abolition of slavery in the District of Columbia, and opposed the Fugitive Slave Law. The account consists of six files under Fessenden Biographical Articles and Addresses in Special Collections.

[8] On Gillet, see also P. J. Staudenraus, *The African Colonization Movement 1816-1865* (New York: Columbia University Press, 1961), 131.

[9] Ibid., 131, 210.

[10] Aaron Chester Adams, *In Memoriam, Rev. David Thurston* (Portland, 1865), comments on "Thurston's antislaveryism" as "not a substitute for the Gospel, but a part of the Gospel" (12-14); Stephen Thurston, *A Discourse on the Erection of a Marble Tablet. . .in Memory of Rev. David Thurston* (Portland, 1871). These items are in the Massachusetts State Library. **William Lloyd Garrison** mentions that he spoke at a New England Anti-Slavery Convention in May 1836, *Letters of William Lloyd Garrison*, vol. 2, 108, 111.

[11] For additional biographical information see Prof. Charles Carroll Everett, D.D., *Leonard Woods, A Discourse. . .Before Bowdoin College and the Maine Historical Society*, Wednesday, July 9, 1879 (Brunswick, 1879). Everett does not explicitly refer to Woods having taken an antislavery position, but makes several allusions to Woods's admiration of and similarity to Daniel Webster, and mentions Woods's belief that patriotism could not be won by artillery fire (29).

5
Bowdoin Faculty Members and Administrators

Alpheus Spring Packard See entry under BOWDOIN ALUMNI.

Egbert C. Smyth See entry under BOWDOIN ALUMNI.

William Smyth See entry under BOWDOIN ALUMNI.

Calvin Ellis Stowe See entry under APPENDIX A.

Thomas Cogswell Upham (Professor of Mental and Moral Philosophy, also Instructor of Hebrew, 1824-67; Professor Emeritus 1867-72) *Birth:* Jan. 30, 1799 Deerfield, NH; *Death:* April 1, 1872 New York, NY, buried in the Bowdoin College Cemetery; *Education:* A.B. Dartmouth 1818, A.M. Dartmouth 1821, student at the Andover Theological Seminary 1821, D.D. Wesleyan 1843, LL.D. Rutgers 1870; *Career:* Instructor of Sacred Literature, Andover Theological Seminary 1821-23; Clergy, Rochester, NH 1823-24; author, poet; *Family:* married Phoebe Moody, May 18, 1825; *Professional and Social Affiliations:* life member of the Colonization Society. (GCB, 37)

References: Biographical File: newspaper article by Eloise M. Jordan entitled "Friend's Beliefs Influenced Author" refers to Upham's home as an underground railroad stop offering protection to runaway slaves en route to Canada; also letter from Upham to Rev. John Orcutt, D.D., April 20, 1870, on African colonization. He refers to the Colonization Society as a noble and divine cause, refers to the slave as being enlightened by civilization but feels that Africans remaining in Africa are "still almost universally in the bondage of ignorance, cruelty and barbarous superstition." For more on Upham, see Alpheus S. Packard, *Address on the Life and Character of Thomas C. Upham, D.D.* (Brunswick, ME: Joseph Griffin, 1873), 19.

John White Chickering (1831-1913), Class of 1852.

General Oliver Otis Howard (1830-1909), Class of 1850.

6
Maine Antislavers

Persons who changed residence during their professional lives are listed beneath the city or town in which they are documented as being associated with antislavery.

AUGUSTA

Bowdoin's Special Collections owns the Records of the Augusta Anti-Slavery Society for 1838. Some of the names therein follow.

James G. Blaine See entry under BOWDOIN ALUMNI.

Richard Drury Rice See entry under BOWDOIN OVERSEERS, TRUSTEES, AND PRESIDENTS

Luther Severance *Birth:* Oct. 26, 1797 Montague, MA; *Death:* Jan. 25, 1855 Augusta, ME; *Education:* No formal higher education; *Career:* Began as journeyman printer in Philadelphia at the Quaker paper Aurora; *National Intelligencer,* Washington, D.C., 1820-23; *Kennebec Journal,* Augusta, ME 1823-25; established himself as an abolitionist and directed his efforts through the *Journal;* Maine Legislature 1830, 1842; Maine State Senate 1835, 1836; U.S. Congress (Liberty Party) two consecutive terms 1843-1847; Diplomatic representative to Havanian Kingdom 1852-54.[1] (BDC, 1795)
References: "Speech of Severence of Maine on the Right of Petition" delivered in House of Representatives, Feb. 16, 1844.

Edward Southwick See entry under BOWDOIN ALUMNI.

Benjamin Tappan See entry under APPENDIX A.

Richard Hampton Vose See entry under BOWDOIN ALUMNI.

BANGOR

In 1832, after speaking in Portland and Hallowell, **William Lloyd Garrison** delivered an anti-colonization lecture in Bangor as the guest of the **Rev. Swan L. Pomeroy,** pastor of the Congregational Church (Schriver, 5). The first annual Bangor Antislavery Society meeting was held in August 1838 with 105 persons in attendance. The Bangor Female Antislavery Society was actively engaged in the national antislavery congressional petitions campaign (Willey, 118, 164). On June 20-22, 1854, the Maine Baptist Anti-Slavery Convention met in Bangor in the First Baptist Church, pastor Rev. S. L. Caldwell (Burrage, 322). Special Collections has the *Records of the Bangor Liberty Association* (1841-43)[2]; this group was associated with antislavery and temperance causes.

Swan L. Pomeroy See entry under BOWDOIN OVERSEERS, TRUSTEES, AND PRESIDENTS.

BRUNSWICK

The first anniversary meeting of the Maine Antislavery Society was held in Brunswick on October 28 and 29, 1838. The actual number of residents who were members of the society is minuscule, but a few were congregants of the First Parish Congregational Church, and some were directly or indirectly affiliated with Bowdoin College. Harriet Beecher Stowe was a resident of Brunswick in 1850, the year her novel *Uncle Tom's Cabin* was published; she later confessed to realizing the death of Uncle Tom in the twenty-third pew of the Church.

George Eliashib Adams See entry under APPENDIX A.

Egbert C. Smyth See entry under BOWDOIN ALUMNI.

William Smyth See entry under BOWDOIN ALUMNI.

Calvin Ellis Stowe See entry under APPENDIX A.

Harriet Beecher Stowe *Birth:* June 14, 1811 Litchfield, CT; *Death:* July 1, 1896 Hartford, CT; *Education:* Student and teacher, Hartford Female Seminary; *Career:* First writings published in

Western Monthly Magazine, 1833; First installment of *Uncle Tom's Cabin* in the *National Era*, 1851; *Uncle Tom's Cabin* published in book form, 1852; wrote several novels and many articles for periodicals (*Uncle Tom's Cabin* the only one that addressed slavery); avoided writing on slavery after *Uncle Tom's Cabin* in opposition to the Fugitive Slave Law of 1850; *Family:* daughter of renowned Calvinist minister Lyman Beecher, brothers Rev. Henry Ward Beecher, Rev. Edward Beecher, sister Catherine Beecher; married **Calvin Ellis Stowe** in Cincinnati January 6, 1836, his second wife; Beecher family moved to Cincinnati, OH 1832; moved to Bowdoin 1850; moved to Andover 1852; upon Calvin Ellis Stowe's retirement, moved to Hartford, CT.

References: Stowe Collection: Letter to Rev. Mr. Bartol (n.d.), re: Rev. Mr. Thomas Strother's (slave) solicitation of "aid to purchase his freedom"; Letter from **Oliver Otis Howard** (Dec. 4, 1878), re: where to locate information on the Freedmens Bureau schools; Letter to Edward Brooks Hall (Sept. 25, 1852), re: solicitation for antislavery ladies, mentions **Frederick Douglass** and James W. C. Pennington; Little Eva's song (adaptation of poem by John Greenleaf Whittier based on character in *Uncle Tom's Cabin*) printed on cloth; recount of her vision of Uncle Tom's death; miscellaneous newspaper clippings—Stowe in Brunswick, in Cincinnati, reception of fiction, etc. Also see the following collections: Oliver Otis Howard Papers, Henry Wadsworth Longfellow Papers; Abbott Memorial Collection—Literary Work, Whittier Tribute Volume, Abbott Memorial Collection—Lyman Abbott Autograph Collection, and Annie Lawrence Edmands Autograph Book.[3]

Thomas Cogswell Upham See entry under BOWDOIN FACULTY MEMBERS AND ADMINISTRATORS.

HALLOWELL

During his Maine tour of 1832, **William Lloyd Garrison** visited Hallowell at the invitation of **Ebenezer Dole, Sr.** (a distant cousin) and **George Shepard** (Schriver, 5). In 1833, the first antislavery society in Maine was organized in Hallowell at the home of Deacon Dole, of Old South Congregational Church. The town hosted the fifth and sixth annual meetings of the Maine Antislavery Society at Old South Church (Feb. 6-7, 1840, and Feb. 4-5, 1841). Hallowell was also the home of several antislavery organs, such as the *Advocate of Freedom* (1838-41), the weekly *Liberty Standard* (1841-48), edited first by **Rev. Joseph Lovejoy** and later by the **Rev. Austin Willey**, who continued as editor when *The Liberty Standard* became *The Free Soil Republican* (1848-49). Hawthorne-Longfellow owns complete runs of the newspaper. Willey was author in 1886 of *The History of Antislavery in State and Nation* (Willey, 119, 156). Special Collections has some materials about the following antislavery locals:

Elias Bond See entry under APPENDIX A.

Ebenezer Dole, Sr. *Birth:* 1776 Newburyport, MA; *Death:* June 9, 1847 Hallowell, ME; *Education:* No formal education mentioned, but served as an apprentice in Newburyport; *Career:* Merchant, ran a storehouse for the poor "in times of scarcity"; *Family:* married Hannah B. Dole; two children, Hannah Dole, Ebenezer Dole, Jr.; distant cousin of **William Lloyd Garrison**.[4]

References: The Dole Family Papers consist of twenty letters to him from his wife, children, and other family members (1815-1845). A letter sent to him from his wife on September 12, 1835, makes reference to the antislavery movement: "Sister Moody says that the abolition system is going down fast here but we must be thankful that it does not hang on men's shoulders." *The Liberty Standard* said of him on June 27, 1847, "Humanity was a part of his religion. He served his God in doing good to man. Goodness was his religion. He labored and saved to give. The chosen objects of his benevolence were the poor and despised, those who were neglected by others. Such a man was sure to be an abolitionist—it could not be otherwise." Willey's *History of Antislavery in State and Nation* cites him as "one of the highest examples of true Christian doctrine" (316-317). This is also exemplified in an angry letter (at the Maine Historical Society) to Dole from a Florida slaveowner, Ambrose Crane, who accused Dole of stealing his Negro servant.

Robert Hallowell Gardiner See entry under APPENDIX A.

Eliphalet Gillet See entry under BOWDOIN TRUSTEES, OVERSEERS, AND PRESIDENTS

George Shepard See entry under BOWDOIN ALUMNI.

Austin Willey *Birth:* 1806; *Death:* Northfield, MN; *Career:* Co-editor with **William Smyth**, *Advocate of Freedom*; Editor, *The Liberty Standard*, which became *The Free Soil Republican* August 31, 1848 (all Maine antislavery papers); Editor, *Portland Inquirer* (Free Soil Party press); author, *History of Antislavery in State and Nation* (1886); advocate for the Liberty Party, attended the Liberty National Convention, 1843; assisted **Samuel Fessenden** in starting the Maine Free Soil Party. (Schriver, 22, 28, 31n-32n, 50-52, 63, 65, 72n)

References: See issues of *Advocate of Freedom* (Oct. 1839-1841) for which he was editor and contributor.

HAMPDEN

Hannibal Hamlin *Birth:* Aug. 27, 1809; *Death:* July 4, 1891 Bangor, ME; *Career:* Lawyer (admitted to the Bar 1833), Hampden 1833-48; Maine State Legislature 1836-40, 1847; Speaker of State House 1837, 1839, 1840; U.S. Congress (Democrat) 1843-47; U.S. Senate (replaced **John Fairfield**) 1848-57 (left the Democratic Party in 1856), 1857-61, 1869-81; Governor (Republican) 1857 (for Jan. and Feb.); Vice President of the U.S. 1861-65; Collector of Port of Boston 1865-66; U.S. Minister to Spain 1881-82; *Professional and Social Affiliations:* Regent, Smithsonian Institution, 1870. (BDAC, 1259)

References: Remarks of Mr. Hamlin, of Maine, Defining his Position, and the Tests of the Cincinnati Convention, in the Senate of the U.S. June 12, 1856 (Washington, D.C.: Congressional Globe, 1856), re: opposition to the repeal of the Missouri Compromise; *Speech . . . in Reply to Gov. Hammond, and in Defence of the North and Northern Laborers* (Washington, D.C.: 1858), re: opposition to the Lecompton Bill and to forms of legislative pressure on the citizens of the Territory of Kansas to admit slavery.[5]

LEWISTON, LIMERICK, OR OXFORD

Charles Freeman See entry under BOWDOIN ALUMNI.

William Pierce Frye See entry under BOWDOIN ALUMNI.

John Jasiel Perry *Birth:* August 2, 1811 Portsmouth, NH; *Death:* May 2, 1897 Portland, ME; *Education:* Maine Wesleyan Seminary; *Career:* Lawyer (admitted to the Bar 1844), Oxford,

Portland 1875-1897; Deputy Sheriff of Oxford County; Maine State Legislature 1840, 1842, 1843, 1872; Maine State Senate 1846, 1847; Clerk of State Legislature 1854; U.S. Congress (Republican) 1855-57, 1859-61; Editor, *Oxford Democratic* 1860-75; Member, State Executive Council 1866, 1867. (BDAC, 1671)

References: *Posting the Books Between the North and the South; Speech in the U.S. House, March 1860* (Washington, D.C.: Nuell & Blanchard [1860]), re: the Constitution does not advocate the existence of slavery nor did the Founding Fathers; *Filibustering Policy of the Sham Democracy* Speech. . . Delivered in the House of Representatives, May 29, 1860 ([Washington, D.C.]: Republican Congressional Committee [1860]), re: against the annexation of Cuba, Mexico, Central America because of their large uneducated populations, and because he believed "The annexation of territory would spread, strengthen, and perpetuate African slavery" (4-8).

Samuel Pickard See entry under APPENDIX A.

PORTLAND

On September 24, 1832, **William Lloyd Garrison** began his Maine tour in Portland. He stayed at the residence of Nathan Winslow, but among his vocal "immediatist" converts was **Samuel Fessenden**. On Wednesday, February 21, 1855, a meeting was held in Portland City Hall to discuss the founding of a new Maine State Colonization Society to function as an auxiliary to the American Colonization Society. The meeting was attended by persons from Brunswick, Portland, Bath, and Bangor. (Schriver, 4-5)

James Appleton See entry under APPENDIX A.

John White Chickering See entry under APPENDIX A.

William Cutter See entry under APPENDIX A.

William Theodore Dwight See entry under BOWDOIN OVERSEERS, TRUSTEES, AND PRESIDENTS.

Samuel Fessenden See entry under BOWDOIN OVERSEERS, TRUSTEES, AND PRESIDENTS.

Icabod Nichols See entry under APPENDIX A.

Albion Keith Parris See entry under APPENDIX A.

SACO, SOUTH BRIDGTON, AND WATERVILLE

Garrison also toured Waterville in 1832 at the invitation of President Rev. Jeremiah Chaplin of Waterville (now Colby) College. His speech provoked the students to form an antislavery society in July 1833. (Schriver, 5)[6]

Jeremiah Chaplin *Birth:* Jan. 2, 1776 Rowley, MA; *Death:* May 7, 1841 Hamilton, NY; *Education:* A.B. Brown University 1799; *Career:* Pastor, Baptist Church, Danvers, MA 1802-18; President, Waterville College, 1821-1833 (resigned due to a conflict with students); Preacher in MA, NY, and CT; *Family:* distant relative of **William Lloyd Garrison**; married Marcia O'Brien; ten children. (WWWA H :170)
References: See sermon at the ordination.

Philip Eastman See entry under APPENDIX A.

John Fairfield See entry under BOWDOIN ALUMNI.

Joseph Palmer Fessenden See entry under BOWDOIN ALUMNI.

WINTHROP

On November 21, 1833, Pastor **David Thurston** preached the first of a series of antislavery sermons on immediate emancipation at the Congregational Church of Winthrop. Several months later, March 4, 1834, a local antislavery society comprising 107 members was founded on the resolve of immediate abolition. Winthrop also organized a Female Antislavery Society and a Juvenile Antislavery Society. (Thurston, 153-55)

Ezekiel Holmes See entry under BOWDOIN ALUMNI.

David Thurston See entry under BOWDOIN OVERSEERS, TRUSTEES, AND PRESIDENTS.

NOTES

[1] Information about Severence's life can be found in **James G. Blaine**'s *Memoir of Luther Severence* (Augusta, ME: Printed at the Office of the Kennebec Journal, 1856).

[2] Contained in volume with *Records of the Bangor Young Men's Association*.

[3] Available in the circulating stacks are the following biographical texts: Charles Edward Stowe, *Harriet Beecher Stowe: The Story of Her Life* (Houghton Mifflin Company: Boston, 1911); Catherine Gilbertson, *Harriet Beecher Stowe* (New York: Appleton-Century Company, Inc., 1937); John Adams, *Harriet Beecher Stowe* (New York: Twayne Publishers, 1963); Noel Bertram Gerson, *Harriet Beecher Stowe: A Biography* (New York: Praeger Publishers, 1976).

[4] Dole also sent Garrison a $100.00 check when he was jailed in Baltimore on libel charges (June 1830) *Letters of William Lloyd Garrison* (Cambridge: Belknap Press of Harvard University Press, 1971), 1:104-107 (Schriver, 18n).

[5] For further information and published correspondence of Hamlin, see *The Life and Public Service of Hon. Abraham Lincoln of Illinois, and Hon. Hannibal Hamlin of Maine* (Boston: Thayer and Eldridge, 1860), 105-128.

[6] Also see Ernest C. Marriner, *The History of Colby College* (Waterville: Colby College Press, 1963), 71-72.

7
Major Figures in Antislavery

The library owns several large collections of correspondence, speeches, manuscripts, and papers by national figures in American antislavery. Materials in Special Collections are complemented by the volumes of works by and about prominent individuals in the movement which are kept in the circulating stacks. See in particular the following collections on the third floor:

LYMAN ABBOTT AUTOGRAPH COLLECTION

This collection contains several letters to Lyman, and some to Edward and Jacob, Abbott from prominent figures in the abolitionist movement. During the Civil War, Lyman Abbott pastored in Terre Haute, Indiana. After the war, he assisted with rebuilding the South, and later edited the *Outlook* (NY) in which he wrote several articles on the Negro's "separate-but-equal" existence in American society. Many of the letters to Lyman Abbott in this collection, as listed below, were written during the era of Reconstruction and post-Reconstruction by Negro educators, commissioners with the Freedmen's Bureau, African missionaries, and formerly strident abolitionists.

Henry Whitney Bellows (1814-1882) During the Civil War, Bellows helped found the U.S. Sanitary Commission, which supervised nurses, supplies, and personal services in military camps and on battlefields. (EWB 1:483)
Reference: Letter to "Rev. & Dr." Lyman Abbott (Oct. 6, 1865): "I am giving all my little leisure to the National Freedmens Relief Commission (not officially)." This message appears on U.S. Sanitary Commission stationery.

John Bigelow (1817-1911) A Free Soil Democrat in the 1840s, and author of a series of letters from *Jamaica in 1850*, Bigelow also wrote a documentary, *France and the Confederate Navy, 1862-68: An International Episode* (1888), which he elaborated in *Lest We Forget* (1905). (DAB II:258-59)

Reference: Letter to Abbott, Dec. 26, 1903, in which he refers to the Civil War as "our struggle with the slaveholders for the preservation of the Union."

Moncure Daniel Conway (1832-1907) Conway wrote several biographies (Paine, Hawthorne, Thomas Carlyle, etc.), founded the *Dial* (1860), and was editor of the *Boston Commonwealth* (1863). Although Conway at one time believed in the inferiority of the Negro, he shifted to an antislavery position, which resulted in his dismissal from the Unitarian Church of Washington, D.C., in 1856. Conway also believed that the Civil War and slavery would have ended if Lincoln had issued the Emancipation Proclamation in 1861. (DAB 4:364-65; WWWA 1:253)

Reference: Letter of March 23, 1891, expresses horror with the New Orleans Massacre,[1] "that these lynchings are nearly always against people of a foreign race or colour, which was by no means the case with the rude frontier courts."

W. E. B. DuBois (1868-1963) Author of numerous historio-sociological studies, such as *The Suppression of the Slave Trade* (1896) and *The Souls of Black Folk* (1903), DuBois was one of the founders of the NAACP and editor of its literary organ *The Crisis* (1910-34). DuBois was a brillant sociologist (Ph.D. Harvard 1895) who served as professor of Latin, Greek, German, and English at Wilberforce (1895-97) and as professor of economics and history at Atlanta (1897-1910). (DANB, 193-99)

Reference: Letter of Jan. 6, 1904 to Lyman Abbott requesting that he speak at the Conference on Race Conditions (in session at the Carnegie Institute, New York City) on the "present situation of the Negro Race." Letter is signed by Kelly Miller and Booker T. Washington as well as DuBois.

William Lloyd Garrison (1805-1879) Most vocal proponent of "moral suasion," Garrison was one of the founders of the Massachusetts Anti-Slavery Society, the New England Anti-Slavery Society, and most importantly, the American Anti-Slavery Society (1833). With colonizationist Benjamin Lundy, he co-edited the *Genius of Universal Emancipation* in Baltimore for one year (1829-30), and then founded his own abolitionist press, the *Liberator* (1831-65), which advocated immediate emancipation. After the Civil War, he continued to work on behalf of the

Negro but through non-organizational channels. (NCAB 2:305-306)[2]

Reference: Letter to Abbott (from Roxbury, Dec. 14, 1867), in which Garrison, due to ill health, declines invitation to deliver lecture "pertaining to the present state of the Freedmen's cause." Also mentions "commencing with the new year my projected History of the Anti-Slavery Struggle." This project was never realized by Garrison.

Horace Greeley (1811-1872) Although opposed to the Kansas-Nebraska Act, the Fugitive Slave Law, and the Dred Scott decision, and supportive of unionism during the Civil War, Greeley favored general amnesty for the South after the War, and even signed a bail bond for the release of Jefferson Davis from the Richmond, VA, prison in 1867. This act blemished his status in the Republican Party. (WWWA:285; NCAB 3:450-52)

Reference: Letter to Abbott (from New York, March 8, 1843), re: places more confidence in the establishment of "Association for *abolishing slavery*, even, than in all the Abolition Lecturers, Abby, included, from Garrison to John Collins."

Rufus Saxton (1824-1908) Saxton, a Republican, advanced from quartermaster to brigadier general to military general of the Department of the South between 1862 and 1865. In 1865, he rose to the brevet rank of brigadier-general in the regular army, and in 1866, he was appointed quartermaster and classified as major. During the War, he was authorized by Stanton to arm and equip 5,000 former slaves, possibly the first official sanction of the employment of black troops. (NCAB 4:219)

Reference: Letter ("Headquarters, Assistant Commissioner, Bureau Refugees, Freedmen and Abandoned Lands, South Carolina, Georgia and Florida," Beaufort, S. C., Aug. 19th, 1865) about the need for agricultural supplies and teachers for the freedmen: "and if we are faithful to the work *now*, in the future these freedmen may in turn send missionaries to enlighten their brothers in Africa."

William H. Seward (1801-1872) Seward lost the Republican presidential nomination in 1860 to Abraham Lincoln, who appointed him U.S. Secretary of State from 1861 to 1869. While serving in the U. S. Senate, Seward urged his colleagues to denounce slavery because of its violation of the "higher law," and to advocate abolition on constitutional grounds. Seward also vehemently opposed the Dred Scott decision. (WWWA:547)

References: Letter (Department of State, Washington, D. C., Nov. 7, 1865) to Executive Committee of the American Union Commission (N. 14 Bible House, New York) declining an initation to speak "at the Cooper Institute. . . for the purpose of setting before the people the wants of the suffering masses in the South and arousing a public interest in measures for their relief and especially for the restoration of industrial and educational systems."

William Tecumseh Sherman (1820-1891) On July 4, 1863, Sherman was appointed brigadier general in the United States Army. He assumed command of the Military Division of Mississippi on March 18, 1864; he captured Atlanta and Savannah, GA, and Columbia, SC, and forced the evacuation of Charleston, SC. On August 12, 1864, he became major general, and rose to the rank of general before he retired from active duty on February 8, 1884. (NCAB 4:32-35)

References: Letter "Head Quarters Military Division of the Mississippi" Saint Louis, Mo., Oct. 27, 1865, to several men in New York, responding with regret to an invitation to speak and "arouse the Citizens of New York on the condition and wants of the people of South left. . . in need by the devastations of the War."

Emery Speer (1848-1918) At age sixteen, Speer enlisted in the Confederate Army. However, in the 1880s, he gained national recognition as the U.S. attorney in Atlanta (appointed by President Arthur) for convicting a horde of Ku Klux Klan members charged with brutally beating Negro voters after an election. With this case, *Ex parte Yarborough* 110 U.S., the Supreme Court established the power of the federal government to protect voters. (NCAB 6:161)

References: Letter to Lyman Abbott (April 21, 1901, on stationery of "Chambers United States Judge, Macon Georgia") from ex-confederate reflecting on upcoming address to the Alumni Society of the University of Georgia at the Centennial Commencement of the institution, in which he intends to admonish his colleagues to progress beyond its sectional views, and embrace the Constitution, the Union, universal education, law and order, and to "stamp out lynching."

Martin Farquhar Tupper (1810-1889) Although he gained his literary reputation with the publication of *Proverbial Philosophy* (1838), which was greatly decried by critics, his "ballads" promoted transatlantic geniality between Britain and America. Tupper was also an early friend to colonization in Liberia, and he gave a gold medal to encourage persons to contribute African literature. (DNB 55)

Reference: Handwritten "The Liberian Church: a sonnet" from Tupper, Feb. 18, 1850.

Booker Talliaferro Washington (1857/58-1913) Washington spent the first nine years of his life as a slave, but after emancipation and the death of his mother, he was forced to make his own living. He earned enough to graduate with honors in 1875 from Hampton Institute. In 1881, General S. C. Armstrong appointed him principal of Tuskegee (which was incorporated as Tuskegee Normal and Industrial Institute in 1892). Washington wielded a great deal of influence among white philanthropists and politicians and was usually approached regarding national issues pertaining to the Negro. In the Preface of *Up From Slavery*, Washington indicates that his relationship with Lyman Abbott was due partly to the serialized publication of "a series of articles, dealing with incidents in my life, which were published consecutively in the *Outlook*." (DANB, 633-36)[3]

References: Several letters to Lyman Abbott, D.D. at the *Outlook* (Tuskegee, A.A., Dec. 22, 1899; South Weymouth, Mass., 3d August, 1903; [Tuskegee, AL] Sept. 10, 1903, on the stationery of Tuskegee Normal and Industrial Institute [Incorporated] For the Training of Colored Young Men and Women), which express gratitude to Abbott for publicizing his book [presumably *Up From Slavery*], and for the editorials on "Negro Graduates"; on these Washington is addressed as "Principal." This collection also contains a typed letter to President Theodore Roosevelt (on personal stationery, Tuskegee Institute, Alabama, Nov. 2, 1908), in which he recounts a recent trip to Mississippi, where he was delighted and surprised "to find many really generous and brave white men and women."

OLIVER OTIS HOWARD COLLECTION

The legacy of Garrisonian and radical abolitionists of antislavery stretches into the early 1900s. The **Oliver Otis Howard** Papers are an invaluable resource for studying the aims and achievements of specific individuals (Northerners and Southerners, former abolitionists and former slaveholders), who, during the Reconstruction and post-Reconstruction era, attempted to bring the Negro closer to full citizenship and participation in American society. Accordingly, the Oliver Otis Howard collection is more than the history of one man's crusade for manumitted slaves through the Freedmen's Bureau. It contains over 100,000 items to and from General Howard. Several correspondents (T. E. Tate, Thomas Conway, Rufus Saxton, etc.) in this collection are also featured in the Lyman Abbott Autograph Collection. Below is just a sampling from this enormous collection of pertinent letters:

Adelbert Ames (1835-1933) Ames served in the Union Army from 1861-65 as lieutenant, colonel, and eventually as brigadier general. On March 15, 1868, he was appointed provisional governor of Mississippi, and to the command of the fourth military district, Department of Mississippi, on March 17, 1869. He served as governor of Mississippi from 1874 to 1876. (Warner, 5-6).
References: Letter of July 12, 1870, to General O. O. Howard asks "the expense of educating and supporting a colored boy at the Howard University," "a friend—a colored boy who wants to go to your University."

Henry Ward Beecher (1813-1887) Rev. Beecher was a very emotional and outspoken advocate of several reforms, including antislavery. He opposed the Compromise of 1850 and proposed northern colonization of Kansas. He campaigned for Fremont and Lincoln, and from 1861-64, he edited the *Christian Union*. (WWWA:117)
Reference: Letter to Edward Stanton (Brooklyn, May 3, 1865), re: the importance of the Freedmen's Bureau, and instilling the virtues of self-help: "the black man is just like the white in this—true he should be [left] and obliged, to take *care* of himself and suffer and enjoy." Beecher also stresses the importance of the shedding of slavery, and the freedmen's acquisition of an

education "to have, in the case of plantation slavery. . . tools, seed, etc."

Salmon Portland Chase (1808-1873) Chase was elected by Free Soilers and Democrats to the U.S. Senate in 1849. Appointed attorney general, he defended the rights of escaped slaves and was dubbed the Attorney General for runaway Negroes. He served as Lincoln's secretary of the treasury during the Civil War. In Oct. 1864 he was appointed chief justice of the U.S. Supreme Court, and presided over the treason trial of Jefferson Davis. On his return to the Senate, he presided over the impeachment of President Johnson. (CDAB, 158-59)

References: Letter of Feb. 8, 1867, partly from J. M. McKim, re: worthy cause educating the freedmen and "the poor of all classes in the South."

Thomas W. Conway (1840-1887) Conway was the district secretary of the National Association for the Education of Colored Ministers and Teachers for Freedmen and was active in the Free Labor movement. In 1864 he was appointed chaplain of the 79th U.S. Colored Infantry. He served as assistant commissioner for freedmen in Louisiana and as State Superintendent of Schools, in which capacity he established 1500 schools for freedmen (see letterhead of correspondence of Oct. 5, 1865, to Lyman Abbott—Head Quarters, Bureau of Refugees, Freedmen & Abandoned Lands in Louisiana). Conway saw his own duty "to assist the work of loyal reconstruction." While General Oliver Otis Howard presided over the Freedmen's Bureau, Conway petitioned Congress to continue to fund the bureau (1868). (Lamb's 2:159)

References: Nine significant letters: Nov. 30, 1865, re: planned travel to England to raise funds to pay freedmen in the South, but cancelled, see Dec. 28, 1865; May 14, 1866, re: current destructive, conservative presidential policy (Andrew Johnson's) regarding activities of the bureau; two chapters about Howard in Conway's *The Great Exodus;* May 24, 1866, and June 8, 1866, re: Conway daily defensive stance in Congress against assaults on Howard's work on behalf of the freedmen, and of his accolades of Howard in a report given to the New York Chamber of Commerce; Feb. 27, 1867, letterhead signifies that Conway is speaking as the District Secretary of the National Association for the Education of Colored Ministers and Teachers for the Freed men; April 26, 1867 re: support bestowed on Gen. Rutherford by loyal black and white officers; Jan. 5, 1868, "I have worked as hard and done as much as anybody (except yourself) to give the poor blacks their full chance in the world which God designed for them as well as us."

Frederick Douglass (ca.1817-1895) An ex-slave and ex-Garrisonian turned political abolitionist, Douglass assisted in recruitment for the 54th and 55th Massachusetts Colored Regiments during the Civil War. In 1871 he served as secretary to the Santo Domingo Commissioners, and was appointed the District of Columbia marshall and recorder of deeds, 1877-86. From 1889 to 1891, Douglass was the U. S. Minister to Haiti. (DANB, 181-86)

References: Letter of July 13, 1870, re: Douglass asserts that he owes his irreverence and disrespect for Christian churches to their failure to "make a stand against slavery," and attributes the success of abolition to secular institutions and nonreligionists; Letter of June 17, 1874, Washington, D.C., on stationery of "Principal Office of the Freedman's Savings and Trust Company," re: remarks on behalf of a poetess who authored a tribute to Charles Sumner which she would like to read the up-coming Sunday at the Congregational Church; Letter of February 18, 1875, Washington, D. C., re: the financial collapse of the Freedmen's Bank; Letter of Oct. 10, 1881, re: response to Francis Fessenden (grandson of **General Samuel Fessenden**) regarding the grandfather's involvement in the abolitionist movement in Portland, ME.

Frederick Douglass, Jr. Son of prominent abolitionist, he met many significant visitors who had come to his home. Among them was John Brown, of whom he has been quoted as saying: "The sun seemed to rise and set to me in John Brown."[4]

References: Letter of Aug. 12, 1871, from Washington, D.C., to Gen. Howard on behalf of the bearer, Mr. Jacob De Witten, "an English Colored Lawyer and shorthand reporter" who needed employment immediately.

Clinton B. Fisk (1823-90) Fisk was a brigadier general during the Civil War, and afterwards served as an assistant commissioner under Howard in the Freedmen's Bureau in Kentucky and Tennessee. He was instrumental in the establishment of Fisk University. (NCAB 6:244)

Reference: Letter of Feb. 21, 1866 re: president's veto of the Freedmen's Bureau Bill.

Henry Highland Garnet (1815-1882) A Presbyterian clergyman and ex-slave, Garnet was educated in the Oneida Institute. A leading abolitionist before the rise of Frederick Douglass, Garnet made history in 1865 as the first black man to deliver a sermon before the House of Representatives. After the Civil War, he worked with the Freedmen's Bureau and in 1882 was appointed minister to Liberia. (DANB, 252-53)
Reference: Letter of March 28, 1867 re: benefits for Mrs. William H. Harris, whose husband enlisted in the army as a "single" freedman.

Edward Everett Hale (1822-1909) Rev. Hale (son of Nathan Hale, and nephew of Edward Everett), pastor of the South Congregational (Unitarian) Church in Boston (1856-99), was a prominent promoter of the "Chautauqua" circles, and wrote several tracts on self-help. He published several articles in the *Atlantic Monthly* in the 1860s. From 1903-1909 he was chaplain of the U.S. Senate. (CDAB, 383)
Reference: Letter of August 11, 1865, from Milton, MA re: request for information about the Freedmen's Bureau from Howard to furnish facts for an article Hale was writing about the bureau for the *North American Review.*

Edgar Ketchum (1840-1905) While Attorney Ketchum was with the Signal Corps, he was made the first lieutenant by brevet for his gallant and meritorious services in the capture of Fort Fisher, NC. (NCAB 4:168, WWWA 1:672).
References: Letter of July 11, 1870, re: Abraham Lincoln's abolition of slavery and the importance of "our treatment of the Freedmen"; letter of July 12, 1870, re: check for $50.00 to the Otey Scholarship fund; letter of July 13, 1870, re: Lincoln and the Emancipation Proclamation, asserts that "Lincoln's glory is the Emancipation. . . .To the glory of the Congress they decided for good to the Negro, and gave all latitude to the Chief Officer of Administration."

C. H. Merwin Merwin was the recording secretary of the Young Men's Christian Association, which elected **Oliver Otis Howard** its president in 1866. Merwin was also the superintendent of the Colored Branch of Canal Mission.

Reference: Letter of Aug. 11, 1871, letterhead "Rooms of the Young Men's Christian Association, Corner of Ninth and D Streets" Washington, D.C.; re: requests Gen. Howard to meet the students of the Canal Missionary Colored School at the Congregational Church on the next Sunday.

Rufus Saxton See entry under Lyman Abbott Autograph Collection.

Reference: Letter of May 24, 1863, Beaufort, SC, re: optimism about the future for the "oppressed," the "vitality in the race" (blacks), and that they "only need to be educated and protected in their rights and all will be well with them."

Charles Sumner (1811-1874) A founder of the Free Soil Party, Sumner served in the Senate from 1851. He was a strong defender of antislavery and delivered many memorable speeches in opposition to the Fugitive Slave Law and the Kansas-Nebraska Act. In 1859, he returned to Congress to deliver his "Barbarism of Slavery" speech, which condemned the institution for moral, economic, and social reasons. (WWWA H:587, and *Works of Charles Sumner,* 15 vols. (Boston: Lee & Shepard, 1875-94).

Reference: Letter of July 15, 1865, Boston, re: a job reference for Co. Pratt, who is "very devoted to the welfare of the freedmen."

Sojourner Truth (ca. 1797-1883) Evangelist and abolitionist, Truth believed she was called by God to testify on behalf of her oppressed race, and against the cruelty they endured under slavery. During the Civil War she aided wounded troops, and afterwards, she petitioned Congress to allocate public lands in the West for newly freed soldiers. (DANB, 605-606).

References: Letter of Dec. 23 [1873], Battle Creek, MI, to "Friend Howard" re: spiritual support, and her latest travels "through Rhode Island Masssachusetts. New York Ohio Michigan Wisconsin Illinois Iowa Missouri Kansas lecturing on my petition and my petition is to get a home for the old colered people emancipated by the war" [sic]; Letter of July 28 [1874], Phoenixville, PA, re: inability to send contribution, requests a copy of a "bill" he authored in honor of her, and mentions her plans to visit "Mrs townsend" in Philadelphia.

NOTES

[1] In the New Orleans Massacre eleven persons were lynched, at least three of whom were Italians. The lynching was precipitated by the murder of a New Orleans police chief who had been investigating the Black Hand and ties to the Mafia (*Encyclopedia of American History*, 284).
[2] There are several biographies of William Lloyd Garrison by his contemporaries and contemporary scholars. Among those by his associates, the library owns Oliver Johnson, *William Lloyd Garrison and His Times; Sketches of the Anti-Slavery Movement in America, and of the Man Who was Its Founder and Moral Leader* (Boston: Houghton, Mifflin and Company, 1881). This book includes an introduction by John Greenleaf Whittier.
[3] The Hawthorne-Longfellow Library owns first editions of all of Booker T. Washington's publications. For more study of Washington's relationship with Lyman Abbott, as well as with Oliver Otis Howard, consult *The Booker T. Washington Papers,* 14 vols., ed. Louis R. Harlan (Chicago: University of Illinois Press, 1972-1989).
[4] Frederic Mary Holland, *Frederick Douglass: The Colored Orator* (New York: Funk & Wagnalls, 1891) 67, 267, 328.

Thomas Cogswell Upham (1799-1872), Professor of Mental and Moral Philosophy.

William Smyth (1797-1868), Class of 1822 and Professor of Natural Philosophy.

Appendix A
Bowdoin and Maine Antislavers: General Holdings

A significant number of Bowdoin and Maine reformers cannot be linked to antislavery by primary documents in Special Collections. Although there are secondary references denoting their antislavery ties, it is not clear whether materials that are still in circulation would make the connection. A search for additional documents might turn up new evidence.

George Eliashib Adams (Overseer 1830-71, Vice President of the Board 1865-71, D.D. 1849) *Birth:* Oct. 27, 1801 Worthington, MA; *Death:* Dec. 25, 1875; *Education:* A.B. Yale 1821, studied at Andover Theological Seminary 1826; *Career:* Professor of Sacred Literature, Bangor Theological Seminary 1827-29; Clergy, First Congregational Brunswick, ME 1829-70, Orange, NJ 1870-75; *Professional and Social Affiliations:* Phi Beta Kappa (Yale), Secretary of the Brunswick Auxiliary Anti-Slavery Society, but considered a moderate on antislavery. (GCB, 5; Clark, 48, 66)

References: Letters in the Chapel Papers, Alpheus Spring Packard Papers, Leonard Woods Papers, Joshua Chamberlain Papers, and Charles Stewart Daveis Papers; three Alumni Pamphlets and a Biographical File. None of these materials mention his antislavery views. Leads may possibly be found in Adams's journal, which is kept in a safe at the First Parish Church in Brunswick (Box 3, no. 13).

James Appleton *Birth:* Feb. 14, 1785; *Death:* August 25, 1862; *Career:* Lieutenant colonel of Gloucester, MA, Regiment; Brigadier general First Brigade 1812; MA Legislature (Gloucester) 1813-14 (one of the first to propose state prohibition of manufacture and distribution of liquor; he also advocated public education, assistance to the poor, and the abolition of slavery); ME General Assembly (Portland) 1836-37; *Family:* married Sarah Fuller; ten children; *Professional and Social Affiliations:* With thirty-six other men from fourteen Maine towns, signed call for convention to form the Maine Anti-Slavery Society, 1834; ran unsuccessfully on Liberty Party ticket for governor of Maine in 1842, 1843, and 1844. (Clark, 43; Schriver, 14, 56; WWWA H:94; Willey, 157, 187).

Reference: Letter to Jesse Appleton, March 21, 1819; no allusion to antislavery.

Elias Bond (A.B. 1837, D.D. 1890) *Birth:* August 19, 1813 Hallowell, ME; *Death:* July 24, 1896 Kohala, Hawaii; *Additional Education:* Bangor Theological Seminary, 1840; *Career:* Mississippi Missionary; American Board of Commissioners for Foreign Missions; went to Kohala, Hawaii, 1840-51; Clergy, native church Kohala, Hawaii, 1851-85; Sugar planter; Founder, Kohala Girls School. *Professional and Social Affiliations:* Athenaean Society (Bowdoin). (GCB, 72; Nason, 166)

References: Two letters between Bond and A. S. Packard, in Packard Papers. See letter of February 24, 1874, which alludes to Professor **William Smyth**. In *Old Hallowell on the Kennebec,* Emma H. Nason mentions Bond as one of the residents of Hallowell who worked laboriously in several reformist causes, among them antislavery: "another noble son of Hallowell who devoted his long life to the work of evangelizing and civilizing the natives of the Hawaiian Islands" (166).

John White Chickering (Overseer 1846-66; D.D. 1855) *Birth:* March 19, 1808 Woburn, MA; *Death:* Dec. 9, 1888 Brooklyn, NY; *Education:* A.B. Middlebury 1826; Andover Theological Seminary 1829; *Career:* Clergy, Bolton, MA 1830-35, High Street Church Portland, ME 1835-65; *Family:* son John W., Jr., Bowdoin 1852; *Professional and Social Affiliations:* Phi Beta Kappa (Middlebury); Secretary, Congressional Temperance Society, Washington, D.C.; Executive Committee, Maine Union in Behalf of the Colored Race; corresponding secretary of the newly organized Maine Colonization Society, 1854. (GCB, 7; Clark, 57, 62, 90, 160-62, 177; Schriver, 35, 40, 41)[1]

References: Three Alumni Pamphlets (sermons) that make no reference to antislavery.

William Cutter (A.B. 1821, Medical School 1821, A.M. 1824, Overseer 1830-41) *Birth:* May 15, 1801 Yarmouth, ME; *Death:* Feb. 8, 1867; *Education:* Andover Theological Seminary 1821-23; *Career:* Merchant, Portland 1823-39; Literary work, New York, NY 1839-46, Bedford, NY 1846-67; *Family:* son of **Levi Cutter**, Overseer 1818-56; married Margaret Dicks, 1828; two sons, two daughters; *Professional and Social Affiliations:* Phi Beta Kappa and Peucinian (both Bowdoin); Member, Executive Committee of

Maine Union in Behalf of the Colored Race. (GCB, 51; Clark, 58, 62)

References: William Cutter to Parker Cleaveland, Portland, July 15, 1828; Commencement Speeches: Valedictory "Oration on the Moral Sublime." No references to antislavery.

John Wallace Ellingwood (A.M. 1824, D.D. 1851, Overseer 1816-60) *Birth:* March 2, 1782 Beverly, MA; *Death:* August 19, 1860; *Education:* A.M. Williams 1816; Andover Theological Seminary 1812; *Career:* Clergy, First or North Church (Congregational) Bath, ME 1812-43; *Professional and Social Affiliations:* Member of the Executive Committee of the Maine Union in behalf of the Colored Race (an antislavery organization not necessarily anti-slaveholders); president, Bath [Colonization] Society; according to Clark, Ellingwood was a moderate who discouraged the Congregational Church from exerting disciplinary action against its Southern churches with slaveowning members. (GCB, 8; Clark, 62, 90, 100, 176)

References: Five speeches and letters in the following collections: Chapel Papers (four letters), Leonard Woods Papers (three letters), Charles S. Daveis Papers (one letter); no references to antislavery stance.

Robert Hallowell Gardiner (Overseer 1811-41, Vice President of the Board 1819-29, President of the Board 1829-41, Trustee 1841-60) *Birth:* Feb. 10, 1782 Bristol, England; *Death:* March 22, 1864; *Education:* A.B. Harvard 1801, J.D. Harvard Law 1806; *Career:* Maine State Legislature 1822; *Professional and Social Affiliations:* Phi Beta Kappa (Harvard); President and charter member, Maine Historical Society; founded the Gardiner Lyceum; erected the Episcopal Church in Gardiner; First treasurer of Maine Antislavery Society, formed in Hallowell, November 18, 1833. Town of Hallowell named after his father, Robert, and the town of Gardiner after him; *Family:* nine children. (Nason, 164; GCB, 10)[2]

References: Letter #17 to Gardiner Oct. 23, 1857, re: his views on **Upham**'s articles of agreement; letter #19 from **William Smyth** (Nov. 26, 1857), re: denominational declaration, Smyth's opinion on majority of orthodox Congregationalists; letter #23 to Gardiner from **John McKeen**, August 11, 1859 re: denominational controversy; article in *Daily Eastern Argus,* August 13, 1910.

Joseph Cammet Lovejoy (A.B. 1829) *Birth:* July 25, 1805 Albion, ME; *Death:* Oct. 19, 1871; *Additional Education:* Bangor Theological Seminary 1831-34; *Career:* Principal, Hallowell Academy 1829-1831; Clergy, Old Town (Orono) 1835-43; Cambridgeport, MA 1843-53; Civil servant, Boston, MA; Editor, *Liberty Standard* (an antislavery organ) 1841-45; *Professional and Social Affiliations:* Phi Beta Kappa and Peucinian Society (both Bowdoin); agent, Maine Temperance Union (1836-41); organizer of a society of boys who adopted a pledge of total abstinence; withdrew from the ministry after allowing a Black husband to sit with his white wife in the front of the church; disapproved of churches that retained members who owned slaves; swayed toward abolitionism by W. L. Garrison; *Family:* brother of Elijah Lovejoy (prominent Ohio antislavery journalist, martyred by an anti-abolitionist mob in 1837), and **Owen**, father, Rev. David Lovejoy, descendant of John Lovejoy, one of the founders of Andover; married Sarah Moody Oct. 6, 1830; eight children. (GCB, 61)

References: Hubbard Family Papers: two letters to John Hubbard dated March 17, 1859, and March 21, 1859; Alumni Pamphlets: "The Law & the Offence: A Lecture on the Subject of Prohibitory Laws in Regard to the Use of Intoxicating Drinks"; "Review of. . . A Lecture on the Subject of Prohibitory Laws in Regard to the Use of Intoxicating Drinks"; "Sermon at the Funeral of Mrs. Eliza Denton on August 28, 1853"; "A Sermon at the Interment of Rev. John Wilder at Cambridgeport [ME], on March 8, 1844."[3] None address antislavery.

Icabod Nichols (Overseer 1810-1817, Trustee 1817-1858, Vice President of the Board 1849-1858, D.D. 1821) *Birth:* July 5, 1784 Portsmouth, NH; *Death:* Jan. 2, 1859 Cambridge, MA; *Education and Honorary Degree:* A.B. Harvard 1802, A.M. Harvard 1805, D.D. Harvard, 1831; *Career:* Pastor, First Church of Portland, ME; *Professional and Social Affiliations:* Phi Beta Kappa (Harvard); one of four vice presidents of the Auxiliary Colonization Society (founded in Portland in 1825).[4] (GCB, 13; Clark, 22)

References: Four speeches, one letter in the Charles S. Daveis Collection; no mention of antislavery.

Albion Keith Parris (A.B. 1806, Overseer 1819-21, Trustee 1821-44) *Birth:* Jan. 19, 1788 Hebron, ME; *Death:* Feb. 11, 1857

Portland, ME; *Education:* A.B. Dartmouth 1806; *Career:* Lawyer, Portland; Massachusetts Legislature 1813; State Senate 1814; U.S. Congress (Democrat) 1815-18; Judge, U. S. District Court of Maine 1818-21; Maine Constitutional Convention 1819; Governor of Maine 1822-26; U.S. Senate 1827-28; Judge, Maine Supreme Court 1828-36; Second comptroller, U.S. Treasury 1836-50; *Professional and Social Affiliations:* Phi Beta Kappa (Dartmouth); Chairman, Maine Colonization Society, which met in Portland, Feb. 21, 1855. (GCB, 13; Schriver, 17)

References: Clara Hawkins Mellen Papers contains two letters from Parris to General Sewall, April 12, 1819, and March 29, 1843, but neither makes reference to slavery or colonization; Hubbard Papers contains one letter of November 8, 1852, regarding a eulogy and observance for the funeral services of Daniel Webster; mentioned in newspaper article.

Samuel Pickard (Overseer 1861-1868) *Birth:* March 9, 1793 Rowley, MA; *Death:* Nov. 2, 1872, Auburn, ME; *Professional and Social Affiliations:* Trustee, Bangor Theological Seminary 1852-72; Manufacturer, Lewiston, ME; one of first ten permanent vice presidents, Maine Anti-Slavery Society. (GCB, 14; Clark, 44, 53).

References: William Willis Papers, letter to William Willis, no allusion to antislavery.

William Smyth See entry under BOWDOIN ALUMNI.

Calvin Ellis Stowe (A.B. 1824; A.M. 1827; Collins Professor of Natural and Revealed Religion 1850-1852) *Birth:* April 26, 1802 Natick, MA; *Death:* August 22, 1886 Hartford, CT; *Further Education:* Andover Theological Seminary 1828; D.D. Indiana University 1837; D.D. Dartmouth 1839; *Career:* Librarian, 1824-25; Instructor, Andover 1828-1830; Professor, Latin and Greek, Dartmouth 1831-1833; Professor, Biblical literature, Lane Theological Seminary 1833-1850; Professor, sacred literature, Andover Theological Seminary 1852-1864; Member, Memorial American Committee for Revision of the English Bible 1872-1874; Religion writer, Hartford, CT 1864-1886; Editor of *Boston Recorder; Professional and Social Affiliations:* Peucinian and Phi Beta Kappa (both Bowdoin); *Family:* married twice: Elizabeth E. Tyler 1831, died in 1834; Harriet Beecher 1836[5]; three daughters and four sons. (GCB, 55; Clark, 166; Schriver, 39)[6]

References: Stowe on the Bible by Calvin Ellis Stowe; letters in the following collections: Bridge-Maurice Papers, Lyman Abbott Autograph Collection, Joshua Lawrence Chamberlain Papers, Captain C. P. Chandler Papers, Chapel Papers, Parker Cleaveland Papers, and William Willis Papers; no allusion to antislavery. Stowe letter to **Horatio Bridge** in Bridge Papers, reveals nothing concerning antislavery (though correspondent connection of significance). Charles Stowe's *Life of Harriet Beecher Stowe* (New York, 1891), records his involvement with his brother-in-law, Henry Ward Beecher, in abetting the safe passage of a fugitive female slave to freedom. Apparently this incident, which occurred in 1839, when the Stowes lived in Cincinnati, provided material for the Eliza story in *Uncle Tom's Cabin* (93).[7]

Benjamin Tappan (Overseer, 1814-65, Vice President of the Board, 1857-65; A.M. 1815, D.D. 1845) *Birth:* Nov. 8, 1788 Newbury, MA; *Death:* Dec. 22, 1863; *Education:* A.B. Harvard 1805, A.M. Harvard 1808, D.D. Colby 1836; *Career:* Tutor, 1809-11; Clergy, Augusta South Church (Congregational) 1820s-60s; *Professional and Social Affiliations:* Phi Beta Kappa (Harvard); Life member, Auxiliary Colonization Society of Maine (joined 1822); Member, Maine Congregational Conference, 1838; Member of the Executive Committee and corresponding secretary, Maine Union in Behalf of the Colored Race; considered a passive abolitionist. Tappan was engaged in a steady output of correspondence with Francis Scott Key of Baltimore, in which the two entertained questions and answers about antislavery. Their exchange was printed in *The Advocate of Freedom* (May 23, 1839), *The African Repository* (April 1839), and the *Augusta Age* (June 11, 1839). (GCB, 15; Clark, 20, 58, 62; Willey, 118; Schriver, 87, 103).

References: Four speeches; most significant is at the Maine Historical Society, article by Thomas Adams (the date and newspaper's name are missing) who remarks: "With the cause of the oppressed he warmly sympathized, though he was not prominently identified with the antislavery movement. It would not be like him to rush into the cause with a headlong zeal that characterized some of its early advocates; yet, I know whereof I affirm when I say, that he cordially sympathized with the movement, though that sympathy was manifested in his usual quiet, prudent way. The simple fact that during an antislavery meeting in Augusta, I dined at his table in company with

Charles Lenox Kanard, shows that he had no sympathy with the inveterate prejudices that prevailed at the time around him."

NOTES

[1] **Chickering**'s antislavery status was questioned by **Samuel Fessenden** and **Austin Willey,** who contended that Chickering was not seriously involved in the movement (Schriver, 35, 40-41).

[2] See biographical profile by Rev. Asa Dalton, "Robert Hallowell Gardiner," *Collections and Proceedings of the Maine Historical Society,* 2nd ser., vol. 1 (Portland: The Society, 1890), 295-99.

[3] **Lovejoy** speaks of Wilder as a man of temperance and abolition principles which "he reduced to practice" (14).

[4] **Garrison** spoke at **Nichols**'s Unitarian Church in Portland on his Maine tour. However, Nichols was absent from the city the night Garrison lectured against the colonization principle: Garrison, *Letters,* vol. 1: #72.

[5] **Calvin Stowe** often accompanied his wife, **Harriet Beecher Stowe,** on speaking trips, and occasionally spoke to crowds, too, for instance the July 4, 1854, convention of female abolitionists at East Livermore, *The Portland Inquirer,* July 13, 1854.

[6] Interesting notes: **Stowe** added the "e" to Stow after his graduation from Bowdoin. While a student at Bowdoin he started a literary society, possibly the Bowdoin Praying Circle, that met in McKeen's store (1815); he made a vow in Faneuil Hall (c. 1850) never to touch his face with a razor again until the Fugitive Slave Law was repealed. Facial hair was not fashionable or accepted. He stayed true to that vow (see Biographical File).

[7] In *The New England Galaxy* 17 (Spring 1976), available at the Maine Historical Society, Stowe is cited as urging the slaves in a moment of excitement to arise and slay the tyrants.

John Searle Tenney (1793-1869), Class of 1816.

Leonard Woods (1807-1878), Fourth President of Bowdoin College.

Appendix B
Journals, Church and Society Reports, and Monographs

Hawthorne-Longfellow Library retains in circulation and in Special Collections invaluable first editions of rare antislavery literature. Below is a bibliography of most of these holdings. These titles are period pieces and not twentieth-century scholarship on antislavery.

JOURNALS

American and Foreign Anti-Slavery Reporter. Vol. 1, no. 1—vol. 1, nos. 23-24 (June 1840—June 1841). New York: American and Foreign Anti-slavery Society.

American Freedmen's Union Commission. *The Freedmen's Record*. Vol. 2, no. 10 (October 1866). Boston: American Freedmen's Union Commission.

The Anti-slavery Examiner. Vol. 1, no. 2 (September 1836). New York: American Anti-slavery Society.

The Anti-slavery Reporter. Vols. 1-5, vol. 6, nos. 1-8 (nos. 1-113) (June 1825-July 1836). London: Printed for the London Society for the Mitigation and Abolition of Slavery in the British Dominions. (Incomplete vols. 2 and 3.)

Boston Recorder. Essays on Slavery: republished from the Boston Recorder and Telegraph for 1825, by Vigornius and others. Amherst, MA: Mark H. Newman, 1826.

The Colonizationist and Journal of Freedom. Apr. 1833-Apr. 1834 monthly, title from caption, July 1833 issue never published. Available on microfilm from University Microfilms (American Periodical Series: 1800-1850).

The Non-Slaveholder. Ed. William J. Allinson. New Series, 1:1853-54. Philadelphia: George W. Taylor, 1853-54.[1]

The Quarterly Anti-slavery Magazine. Vol. 1, no.1 (Oct. 1835). New York: American Anti-slavery Society.

A Voice From the Jail. Vol. 1, no.1 (Dec. 11, 1842). Newburyport, MA: Thomas Parnell Beach.

CHURCH AND SOCIETY REPORTS AND PROCEEDINGS

American Anti-slavery Society. *Annual Report of the American Anti-slavery Society: for the year ending May 1, 1860, by the Executive Committee.* New York: American Anti-slavery Society, 1861.

American Colonization Society. *Annual Reports of the American Society for Colonizing the Free People of Color of the United States.* 91 vols. in 7 vols.

———. *Information about Going to Liberia: with Things which Every Emigrant Ought to Know; Report of Messrs. Fuller and Janifer: Sketch of The History of Liberia: and the Constitution of the Republic of Liberia.* Washington: American Colonization Society, 1852.

American Society for Colonizing the Free People of Colour of the United States. *The Sixth Annual Report of the American Society for Colonizing the Free People of Colour of the United States.* Washington City: Davis and Force, 1823.

Anti-slavery Convention. *Proceedings of the Anti-slavery Convention: assembled at Philadelphia, December 4, 5, and 6, 1833.* New York: Dorr & Butterfield, 1833.

Anti-Slavery Convention of American Women. *Turning the World Upside Down or [Minutes of the Convention].* New York, 1837.

Anti-Slavery and Aborigines' Protection Society. *Slavery in Europe; a Letter to Neutral Governments from the Anti-Slavery Society.* London: Hodder & Stoughton, 1917.

Boston Female Anti-slavery Society. *Report of the Boston Female Anti-slavery Society, with a concise statement of events, previous and subsequent to annual meetings of 1835*. 2d ed. Boston: Boston Female Anti-slavery Society, 1836.

Broadway Tabernacle Anti-slavery Society. *Proceedings of a Meeting to Form the Broadway Tabernacle Anti-slavery Society, with the Constitution: and Address to the Church.* New York: William S. Dorr, 1838.

Church Anti-slavery Society. *Proceedings of the Convention Which Met at Worcester, MA, March 1, 1859.* New York: John F. Trow, 1859.

Committee of Vigilance, Boston. *Address of the Committee Appointed to a Public Meeting Held at Faneuil Hall, Sept. 24, 1846, for the Purpose of Considering the Recent Case of Kidnapping: with an Appendix [Committee of Vigilance; chairman Samuel G. Howe].* Boston: White & Potter, 1846.

Convention for the Improvement of the Free People of Color. *Minutes and proceedings of the First Annual Convention of the People of Color: held by adjournments in the city of Philadelphia from the sixth to the eleventh of June, inclusive, 1831.* Philadelphia: published by order of the Committee of Arrangements, 1831.

Convention of Congregational Ministers of Massachusetts. *Report of the Committee on Slavery to the Convention of Congregational Ministers of Massachusetts: presented May 30, 1849.* Boston: Press of T.R. Marvin, 1849.

Friends, Society of. *The Appeal of the Religious Society of Friends in Pennsylvania, New Jersey, Delaware, etc., to their fellow citizens of the United States: on behalf of the coloured races.* Philadelphia: Friends' Book-store, 1858. Or [Lea, Henry Charles. *Bible Views of Polygamy.* Bound with: *The Appeal of the Religious Society of Friends...on Behalf of the Colored Races.* Philadelphia: Friends' Bookstore, 1858.]

———. *New England Yearly Meeting. Meeting for Sufferings, Testimony of the Religious Society of Friends against slavery: revived by the representatives of New England Yearly Meeting.* Boston: S. N. Dickinson & Co., 1847.

———. *Philadelphia Yearly Meeting. A Brief Statement of the Rise and Progress of the Testimony of the Religious Society of Friends, Against Slavery and the Slave Trade.* Philadelphia: Joseph and William Kite, 1843.

Massachusetts. [State Anti-Texas Committee.] *Report of the Massachusetts Committee to Prevent the Admission of Texas as a Slave State.* [s.l. : s.n., 1845].

Massachusetts Abolition Society. *The Second Annual Report of the Massachusetts Abolition Society, together with the proceedings of the second annual meeting, held at Tremont Chapel, May 25, 1841.* Boston: David H. Ela, 1841.

Massachusetts Anti-Slavery Society. Board of Managers. *Annual report of the Board of Managers of the Massachusetts Anti-Slavery Society, with some account of the annual meeting.* Boston: Isaac Knapp, 1836-1842.

———. Board of Managers. *Annual report presented to the Massachusetts Anti-Slavery Society by its Board of Managers, 11th (Jan. 25, 1843)—21st (Jan. 26, 1853).* Boston: The Society, 1843-1853.

———. *Proceedings of the Massachusetts Anti-slavery Society, at its Seventh Annual Meeting, Held in Boston, Jan. 23, 1838.* Boston: The Society [1838].

National Anti-slavery Bazaar. *Report of the twenty-fourth national anti-slavery festival.* Boston: Printed for the managers, 1858.

New England Anti-slavery Convention. *Proceeding of the fourth New England Anti-slavery Convention, held in Boston, May 30, 31, and June 1 and 2, 1837.* Boston: Isaac Knapp, 1837.

New York Young Men's Anti-slavery Society. *Preamble and constitution of the New York Young Men's Anti-slavery society, formed May 2, 1834.* New York: W. T. Coolidge & Co., 1834.

A Retrospective View of West India Slavery. Together with its present aspect, submitted at a public meeting of the Hibernian Negroes'

Friend Society, to which are added, a chronicled detail of the late insurrection in Jamaica, and other facts illustrative of the subject, drawn from authentic sources. Dublin: P. Dixon Hardy, 1832.

Rhode Island Anti-slavery Convention. *Proceedings of the Rhode Island anti-slavery convention, held in Providence on the 2nd, 3rd, and 4th of Feb., 1836*. Providence: H. H. Brown, 1836.

Union State Central Committee. *Immediate emancipation in Maryland, proceedings of the Union State Central Committee, at a meeting held in Temperance Temple, Baltimore, Wednesday, December 16, 1863*. Baltimore: Bull & Tuttle, 1863.

United States Congress, House of Representatives, Select Committee on Emancipation and Colonization. *Report of the Select Committee on Emancipation and Colonization, with an appendix*. Washington: Government Printing Office, 1862.

Worcester Central Conference of Congregational Churches. *Resistance to Slavery Every Man's Duty, a report on American slavery, read to the Worcester Central Association, March 2, 1847*. Boston: Wm. Crosby & H. P. Nichols, 1847.

MONOGRAPHS

Adams, Charles Francis. *Texas and the Massachusetts Resolutions*. Boston: Eastburn's Press, 1844.

———. *What Makes Slavery a Question of National Concern: a lecture delivered, by invitation, at New York, January 30, and at Syracuse, February 1, 1855*. Boston: Little, Brown, and Co., 1855.

An Address to Christians of all Denominations on the Inconsistency of Admitting Slave-holders to Communion and Church Membership. Philadelphia: S. C. Atkinson, printer, 1831.[2]

Africans Taken in the Amistad. Congressional Document, Containing the Correspondence, & c., in relation to the Captured Africans. New York: Antislavery, 1840.

Allen, Isaac. *Is Slavery Sanctioned by the Bible?: a premium tract.* Boston: American Tract Society, 1860.

Antislavery Tracts, published by the American Anti-Slavery Society (New York, n.d. [185?-186?]): No. 1: *The United States Constitution*; No. 2: *White Slavery in the United States* ; No. 4: Rev. T. W. Higginson, *Does Slavery Christianize the Negro?*; No. 5: Daniel O'Connell, *Extracts of Speeches from...Upon American Slavery: with other Irish Testimonies* (1860); No. 14: *A Fresh Catalogue of Southern Outrages upon Northern Citizens* (1860); No. 19: Charles King Whipple, *Relations of Anti-Slavery to Religion* (1856).

Appeal of Clerical Abolitionists on Anti-slavery Measures; reply/ by editor pro. tem. of the Liberator; a layman's reply to a clerical appeal; reply to the appeal/ by A. A. Phelps; declaration of abolitionist in the theological seminary at Andover, MA. Boston: The Liberator, 1837.

Ashmun, Jehudi. *History of the American Colony in Liberia, from December 1821 to 1823; compiled authentic records of the colony.* Washington City: printed by Way & Gideon, 1826.

Bartlett, D. W. *The Life and Public Services of Abraham Lincoln, with a Portrait on Steel. To which is Added a Biographical Sketch of Hon. Hannibal Hamlin [of Maine].* New York: H. Dayton, Publisher, 1860.

Birney, James Gillespie. *The American Churches: The Bulwarks of American Slavery.* 2d American ed. Newburyport: Charles Whipple, 1842.

———. *The American Churches: The Bulwarks of American Slavery.* 3d American ed. Concord, N. H.: Parker Pillsbury, 1885.

Blair, Montgomery. *Supreme Court of the United States. No. 7—December Term, 1856. Dred Scott, (a Colored Man) vs. John F. A. Sanford: Argument of Montgomery Blair, of Counsel for the Plaintiff in Error.* Washington, D.C.: Gideon, printer [1856].

Bourne, George. *Condensed Anti-slavery Bible Argument, by a Citizen of Virginia.* New York: S. W. Benedict, 1845.

Bowyer, Robert. *Abolition of the Slave Trade. Mr' Bowyer's Proposal to Publish a Tribute of the Fine Arts in Honour of this Interesting Event.* London: T. Beasley [18??].

Brook, Samuel. *Slavery and the Slaveholder's Religion: As Opposed to Christianity.* Cincinnati: published by author, 1846.

Brown, John. *The Life and Letters of John Brown, Liberator of Kansas, and Martyr of Virginia.* Ed. F. B. Sanborn. Boston: Roberts Brothers, 1891.

Brown, William Wells. *Narrative of William W. Brown, A Fugitive Slave.* Boston: At the Antislavery Office, 1847.

Channing, William Ellery. *An Address Delivered at Lenox, on the first of August, 1842, the Anniversary of Emancipation in the British West Indies.* Lenox, MA: J. G. Stanly, 1842.[3]

———. *The Duty of Free States, or, Remarks, Suggested by the Case of the Creole.* Boston: William Crosby & Company, 1842.

———. *Slavery*, 3d ed., rev. Boston: James Munroe and Co., 1836.

Chase, Salmon Portland. *Union and Freedom, Without Compromise: speech of Mr. Chase, of Ohio, on Mr. Clay's compromise resolutions: in Senate, March 26, 1850.* Washington: Buell & Blanchard, 1850.

Chickering, Jesse. *Letter Addressed to the President of the United States on Slavery.* Boston: Redding and Company, 1855.

Child, David Lee. *Rights and Duties of the United States Relative to Slavery Under the Laws of War: no military power to return any slave: "contraband of war" inapplicable between the United States and their insurgent enemies.* Boston: R. F. Wallcut, 1861.

Child, L. Maria. *Isaac T. Hopper: A True Life.* Boston: John P. Jewett & Co., 1853.

———. *The Patriarchal Institution as Described by Members of Its Own Family*. New York: American Anti-slavery Society, 1860.

———. *The Right Way the Safe Way: proved by emancipation in the British West Indies, and elsewhere*. New York: published and for sale at 5 Beekman Street, 1862.

Clarkson, Thomas. *An Essay on the Slavery and Commerce of the Human Species, Particularly the African; Translated from a Latin Dissertation, which was Honoured with the First Prize in the University of Cambridge, for the Year 1785*. London: J. Phillips, 1788.

———. *The History of the Rise, Progress, and Accomplishment of the Abolition of the African Slave Trade by the British Parliament*. 3 vols. New York: John S. Taylor, 1836.[4]

Clowes, William Laird. *Black America: A Study of the Ex-slave and his Late Master*. Repr., with large additions, from "The Times." London: Cassell, 1891.

The Constitution of a Pro-slavery Compact, or, Selections from the Madison Papers. 2d ed., enl. New York: American Anti-slavery Society, 1845.

Corwin, Thomas. *Free Soil vs. Slavery: speech of Mr. Corwin, of Ohio, against the compromise bill: delivered in the Senate of the United States, Monday, July 24, 1848*. Washington: Buell & Blanchard, 1848.

Cromwell, John W. *The Early Negro Convention Movement*. Washington: The Academy, 1904.

Dexter, Henry Martyn. *Our National Condition and its Remedy: a sermon preached in the Pine Street Church, Boston, on Sunday, June 22, 1856*. Boston: John P. Jewett & Co., 1856.

Dickinson, John. *A Serious Address to the Rulers of America, on the Inconsistency of their Conduct Respecting Slavery; Forming a Contrast Between the Encroachments of England on American*

Liberty and American Injustice in Tolerating Slavery. London: J. Phillips, 1783.

Douglass, Frederick. *My Bondage and My Freedom.* New York and Auburn: Miller, Orton & Mulligan, 1855.

Drisler, Henry. *A Reply to the "Bible View of Slavery, by J. H. Hopkins, D.D., Bishop of the Diocese of Vermont."* New York: C. S. Wescott & Co., 1863.

Emerson, Ralph Waldo. *An Address Delivered in the Court-house in Concord, Massachusetts, on 1st August, 1844: on the anniversary of the emancipation of the negroes in the British West Indies.* Boston: James Munroe and Company, 1844.

The Equality of All Men Before the Law: claimed and defended/ in speeches by William D. Kelley, Wendell Phillips, and Frederick Douglass; and letters from Elizur Wright and Wm. Heighton. Boston: Press of Geo. C. Rand & Avery, 1865.

Fee, John Gregg. *Non-fellowship with Slaveholders: the Duty of Christians.* New York: John A. Gray, 1855.

Fitch, Graham Newell. *The Slave Question: speech of Hon. Graham N. Fitch, of Indiana, in the House of Representatives, February 14, 1850: in Committee of the whole on the state of the Union, on the resolution referring the President's message to the various standing committees.* Washington: Congressional Globe Office, 1850.

Foster, Stephen Symonds. *The Brotherhood of Thieves, or, A True Picture of the American Church and Clergy: a letter to Nathaniel Barney.* Concord, NH: Parker Pillsbury, 1886.

Fowler, Orin. *Slavery in California and New Mexico: speech of Mr. Orin Fowler, of Massachusetts, in the House of Representatives, March 11, 1850.* Washington: Buell & Blanchard, 1850.

Garrison, William Lloyd. *An address delivered before the free people of color: in Philadelphia, New York, and other cities, during the* month of June, 1831. Boston: Stephen Foster, 1831.

———. 'No Fetters in the Bay State': speech of Wm. Lloyd Garrison, before the Committee on Federal relation, in support of the petitions asking for a law to prevent the recapture of fugitive slaves: Thurs., Feb. 24, 1859, phonographic report by Jas. M. W. Yerrington. Boston: R. F. Wallcut, 1859.

———. West India Emancipation: a speech delivered at Abington, MA, on the first day of August, 1854, phonographic report by J. M. W. Yerrington. Boston: American Anti-Slavery Society, 1854.

Gerry, Elbridge. Speech of Mr. Gerry, of Maine, on the slavery question: delivered in the House of Representatives, May 21, 1850. Washington: Congressional Globe Office, 1850.

Giddings, Joshua Reed. History of The Rebellion: Its Authors and Causes. New York: Follett, Foster & Co., 1864.

———. Slavery in the Territories: speech of Hon. J. R. Giddings, of Ohio, in the House of Representatives, Mon., March 18, 1850, in Committee of the whole on the state of the Union, on the President's message transmitting the Constitution of California. Washington: Buell & Blanchard, 1850.

———. Speeches in Congress. Boston: John P. Jewett & Company, 1853.[5]

Gilmore, James [pseud. Edmund Kirke]. Among the Pines, or South in Secession-Time. New York: J. R. Gilmore, 1862.

Goodell, William. The American Slave Code in Theory & Practice: Its Distinctive Features shown by Its Statutes, Judicial Decisions, and Illustrative Facts. New York: American and Foreign Anti-Slavery Society, 1853.[6]

Goodloe, Daniel Reaves. The Southern Platform, or, Manual of Southern Sentiment on the Subject of Slavery. Boston: John P. Jewett & Co., 1858.

Green, Beriah. *Things for Northern Men to Do: A Discourse (Delivered Lord's Day Evening, July 17, 1836 in the Presbyterian Church, Whitesboro, N.Y.).* New York, 1836.

Gregoire, M. *De la traité et de l'esclavage des noirs et des blancs, par un ami des hommes de toutes les couleurs.* Paris: Adrien Egron, imprimeur, 1815.

Gregory, John. *The Life and Character of John Brown: a sermon preached at the Wesleyan Methodist Church, Pittsburgh, PA, on Sunday evening Dec. 4, 1859.* Pittsburgh: A. A. Anderson, 1860.

Grimke, Angelina Emily. *Appeal to the Christian Women of the South.* 3d ed., rev. and corr. [Shrewsbury, NJ: 1836].[7]

———. *Letters to Catherine E. Beecher: in reply to an essay on slavery and abolitionism.* Boston: Isaac Knapp, 1838.

Hall, Nathaniel. *The Moral Significance of the Contrasts Between Slavery and Freedom: a discourse preached in the First Church, Dorchester, May 10, 1864.* Boston: Walker, Wise, and Company; Ebenezer Clapp, 1846.

———. *Two Sermons on Slavery and its Hero-victim.* Boston: John Wilson, 1859.

Haviland, Laura S. *A Woman's Life Work: Including Thirty Years' Service on the Underground Railroad and in the War.* 5th ed. Grand Rapids, MI: S. B. Shaw, 1881.

Is Slavery A Blessing?: a reply to Prof. Bledsoe's Essay on Liberty and Slavery, with remarks on slavery as it is, by a citizen of the South. Boston: John P. Jewett & Co., 1857.

Jackson, Francis. *Letter from Francis Jackson.* Boston: Andrews, Prentiss, & Studley, 1844.

Jay, William. *A View of the Action of the Federal Government in Behalf of Slavery.* New York: American Anti-Slavery Society, 1839.

Kingsbury, Harmon. *The Slavery Question Settled: Man-stealing, Legitimate Servitude, etc.* New York: John A. Gray, 1862.

Kramer, John Theophilus. *The Slave-auction.* Boston: Robert F. Wallcut, 1859.

Lieber, Francis. *Plantations for Slave Labor: the Death of the Yeomanry* [s.l. : s.n., 186?].

Lundy, Benjamin. *The War in Texas; A Review of Facts and Circumstances, Showing that This Contest is A Crusade against Mexico, set on Foot and Supported by Slaveholders, Land-Speculators, &c. in order to Re-establish, Extend, and perpetuate the System of Slavery and the Slave Trade.* 2d ed., rev. and enl., Philadelphia: Merrihew and Gunn, 1837.

Lundy, John Patterson. *Review of Bishop Hopkins' Bible View of Slavery, by a presbyter of the church of Philadelphia.* Philadelphia: s.n., 1863.

Mann, Horace. *Speech of Horace Mann, of Massachusetts, on the subject of slavery in the territories, and the consequences of a dissolution of the Union: delivered in the United States House of Representatives, Feb. 15, 1850.* Boston: Redding and Company, 1850.

May, Samuel Joseph. *A Discourse on Slavery in the United States, delivered in Brooklyn, CT, July 3, 1831.* Boston: Garrison and Knapp, 1832.

———. *Memoir of Samuel Joseph May.* Ed. Thomas James Mumford. Boston: Roberts Brothers, 1873.

———. *Some Recollections of Our Antislavery Conflict.* Boston: Fields, Osgood, & Co., 1869.

———. *Speech of Samuel J. May, to the Convention of Citizens of Onondaga County, in Syracuse on the 14th of Oct., 1851, called "to consider the principles of the American government, and the extent to which they are trampled under foot by the Fugitive Slave*

Law": occasioned by an Attempt to Enslave an Inhabitant of Syracuse. Syracuse: Agan & Summers, 1851.

Miner, Charles. *Speech of Mr. Miner of Pennsylvania, delivered in the House of Representatives on Tues. and Wed., Jan 6 & 7, 1829, on the Subject of Slavery and the Slave Trade in the District of Columbia, with notes.* Washington: Gales and Seaton, 1829.

Newhall, Fales Henry. *The Conflict in America: a funeral discourse occasioned by the death of John Brown of Ossawattomie, who entered into rest, from the gallows, at Charlestown, VA, Dec. 2, 1859, preached at Warren St. M. E. Church, Roxbury, Dec. 4.* Boston: J. M. Hewes, 1859.

Newman, Louis C. *The Bible View of Slavery Reconsidered, a Letter to the Right Rev. Bishop Hopkins.* 2d ed., rev. and somewhat enl. Philadelphia: Henry B. Ashmead, 1863.

Niles, John Milton. *Speech of Mr. Niles, of Connecticut, on the Petition of a Society of Friends in Pennsylvania, praying for the abolition of slavery in the District of Colombia, in Senate, Feb. 15, 1836.* Washington: Blair & Rives, 1836.

Palfrey, John Gorham. *Speech of Mr. Palfrey, of Massachusetts, on the political aspect of the slave question, delivered in the House of Representatives, Jan. 26th, 1848.* Washington: J. & G. S. Gideon, 1848.

Papers Relating to the Garrison Mob. Ed. Theodore Lyman, 3rd. Cambridge: Welch, Bigelow, and Company, 1870.

Parker, Theodore. *The Boston Kidnapping, a Discourse to Commemorate the Rendition of Thomas Simms [i.e. Sims], delivered on the first anniversary thereof, April 12, 1852, before the Committee of Vigilance, at the Melodeon in Boston.* Boston: Crosby, Nichols, & Company, 1852.

_____. *Some Thoughts on the New Assault Upon Freedom in America, and the general state of the country in relation thereunto, set forth in a discourse preached at the Music Hall, in Boston, on*

Monday, Feb. 12, 1854. Boston: Benjamin B. Mussey & Co., 1854.

———. *The Trial of Theodore Parker for the "Misdemeanor" of a Speech in Faneuil Hall Against Kidnapping, Before the Circuit Court of the United States, at Boston, April 8, 1855, with the Defence of Theodore Parker.* Boston: Published by the Author, 1855.

Pearl, Cyril. *Remarks on African Colonization and the Abolition of Slavery, in two parts, by a citizen of New England.* Windsor, VT: Richards & Tracy, 1833.

Phillips, Wendell. *Speech of Wendell Phillips, at the Worcester Disunion Convention, Jan. 15, 1857.* Boston: printed for the American Anti-slavery Society, 1857.

———. *The War for the Union.* New York: John B. Alden, Publisher.[8]

Pillsbury, Parker. *Act of the Antislavery Apostles.* Concord, NH: Clague, Wegman, Schlight & Co., 1883.[9]

———. *The Church as It is: or the Forlorn Hope of Slavery.* Boston: A. Forbes, Printer, 1847.

Putnam, Alfred Porter. *A Discourse on William Lloyd Garrison and the Anti-Slavery Movement delivered at The Church of the Saviour, Brooklyn, N.Y., Sunday Evening, June 1, 1879.* Brooklyn: Tremlett & Co., 1879.

Quincy, Josiah. *Address Illustrative of the Nature and Power of the Slave States, and the Duties of the Free States, delivered at the request of the inhabitants of the town of Quincy, MA, on Thurs., June 5, 1856, altered and enlarged since delivery.* Boston: Ticknor and Fields, 1856.

———. *Remarks on the Letter of the Hon. Rufus Choate to the "Whig State Committee of Maine," Written in Answer to a Letter of the Hon. John Z. Goodrich.* Quincy [MA], 1856.

Ranking, John. *Letters on American Slavery, addressed to Mr. Thomas Rankin*. Boston: Garrison and Knapp, 1833.[10]

Redpath, James. *The Public Life of Capt. John Brown*. Boston: Thayer and Elridge, 1860.[11]

Remarks on the Demoralizing Influence of Slavery, by a Resident of the Cape of Good Hope. London: printed by Bagster and Thoms for the Society for the Mitigation and Gradual Abolition of Slavery throughout the British Dominions, 1828.

Remarks on Slavery and Emancipation. Boston: Hillard, Gray, & Co., 1834.

Root, David. *The Abolition Cause Eventually Triumphant, a sermon delivered before the Anti-slavery Society of Haverhill, MA, Aug., 1836*. Andover: Gould and Newman, 1836.

Sanford, S. P. *Poem Suggested by A. F. Biard's Picture of a Slave Mart*. Boston: Twelfth National Anti-slavery Bazaar [1850].

Schurz, Carl. *The Condition of the South, extracts from the report of Major-General Carl Schurz on the states of South Carolina, Georgia, Alabama, Mississippi, and Louisiana, addressed to the President*. Washington: s.n., 1866.

Sherwood, Henry Noble. *Early Negro Deportation Projects*. Reprinted from *Mississippi Valley Historical Review* 11 (March) 1916.

Shipherd, Jacob R., compiler. *History of the Oberlin-Wellington Rescue*. Boston: John P. Jewett and Company, 1859.

Sims, Thomas, respondent. *Trail of Thomas Sims, on an issue of personal liberty, on the claim of James Potter, of Georgia, against him, as an alleged fugitive from service, arguments of Robert Rantoul, Jr., and Charles G. Loring, with the decision of George T. Curtis, Boston, April 7-11, 1851, phonographic report by Dr. James W. Stone*. Boston: W. S. Damrell & Co., 1851.

Sloane, James Renwick Wilson. *Review of Rev. Henry J. Van Dyke's discourse on "The character and influence of abolitionism", a sermon preached in the Third Reformed Presbyterian Church...on Sabbath evening, Dec. 23, 1860.* New York: William Erving, 1861.

Smart, Ephraim Knight. *Speech of Hon. E. K. Smart, of Maine, in defence of the North against the charge of aggression upon the South, delivered in the House of Representatives, April 23, 1852.* Washington: printed at the Congressional Globe Office, 1852.

Smectymnus, pseud. *19th cent. Slavery and the Church, two letters addressed to Rev. N. L. Rice, D.D., in reply to his letters to the Congregational deputation, on the subject of slavery, also a letter to Rev. Nehemiah Adams, D.D., in answer to the "South side view of slavery."* Boston: Crocker and Brewster, 1856.

Smith, Francis Ormand Jonathan. *The Uniform Record of all Political Parties in Maine, down to 1856, in opposition to human slavery, speech of Hon. Francis O. J. Smith, to the Republican state convention, Portland, July 8, 1856.* Bangor: Maine Expositor, 1856.

Smith, Gerrit. *Abstract of the Argument on the Fugitive Slave Law, made by Gerrit Smith, in Syracuse, June, 1852, on the trial of Henry W. Allen, U.S. Deputy Marshal, for kidnapping.* Syracuse: Daily Journal, 1852.

———. *Controversy Between New York Tribune and Gerrit Smith.* New York: John A. Gray, 1855.

———. *No Treason in Civil War, a speech of Gerrit Smith at Cooper Institute, New York, June 8, 1865.* New York: American News Company, 1865.

———. *Personal Liberty Law, a speech of Gerrit Smith, Feb. 6, 1861, in the Capitol before the Judiciary Committees of the New York Legislature.* New York: New York Daily Tribune, 1861.

———. *Speeches of Gerrit Smith in Congress.* New York: Mason Brothers, 1856.[12]

Spooner, Lysander. *The Unconstitutionality of Slavery*. Boston: Bela Marsh, 1856.

Stevens, Charles Emery. *Anthony Burns; A History*. Boston: John P. Jewett and Company, 1856.

Stewart, Alvan. *Writings and Speeches of Alvan Stewart, on Slavery*. Ed. Luther Rawson Marsh. New York: A. B. Burdick, 1860.

Still, William. *The Underground Railroad; a Record of Facts, Authentic Narratives, Letters, &c. Narrating the Hardships Hair-Breadth Escapes and Death Struggles of the Slaves in their Efforts for Freedom, as Related by Themselves and Others, or Witnessed by the Author; Together with Sketches of Some of the Largest Stockholders, and Most Liberal Aiders and Advisers of the Road*. 1872.

Stroyer, Jacob. *Sketches of My Life in the South*, pt. I. Salem: Salem Press, 1879.

Stuart, Charles. *Immediate Emancipation, safe and profitable for masters—happy for slaves—right in government—advantageous to the nation—would interfere with no feelings but such as are destructive—cannot be postponed without continually increasing danger, an outline for it, and remarks on compensation, reprinted from the (Eng.) Quarterly magazine and review, for April, 1832*. Newburyport: published by Charles Whipple, 1838.

Substance of a Speech Intended to have been made on Mr. Wilberforce's Motion for the Abolition of the Slave Trade. London, 1792.

Sumner, Charles. *Argument of Charles Sumner, Esq. against the constitutionality of separate colored schools, in the case of Sarah C. Roberts vs. the City of Boston before the Supreme Court of Massachusetts, Dec. 4, 1849*. Boston: B. F. Roberts, 1849.

_____. *The Barbarism of Slavery, speech of Hon. Charles Sumner on the bill for the admission of Kansas as a free state, in the United States Senate, June 4, 1860*. Washington, D.C.: Thaddeus Hyatt, 1860. Or New York: Young Men's Republican Union, 1863.

———. *The Crime Against Kansas. The Apologies for the Crime. The True Remedy. Speech of Hon. Charles Sumner, in the Senate of the United States, 19th and 20th May, 1858*. Washington, D.C.: Buell & Blanchard, printers, 1856.

———. *Freedom National, Slavery Sectional, speech of Hon. Charles Sumner, of Massachusetts, on his motion to repeal the Fugitive Slave Bill, in the U.S. Senate, Thursday, August 26, 1852*. [s.l. : s.n., 1852].

———. *Slavery and the Rebellion: One and Inseparable, speech of Hon. Charles Sumner, before the New York Young Men's Republican Union, at Cooper Institute, New York, on the afternoon of November 5, 1864*. Boston: Wright & Potter, 1864.

———. *White Slavery in the Barbary States, a lecture before the Boston Mercantile Library Association, Feb. 17, 1847*. Boston: William D. Ticknor and Company, 1847.

Sunderland, La Roy. *Anti-Slavery Manual, Containing a Collection of Facts and Arguments on American Slavery*. New York: Piercy & Reed, 1837.

Talbot, Thomas H. *An Argument on the "Fugitive Slave Act."* Boston: Bela Marsh, 1852.

Tappan, Benjamin. *Remarks of Mr. Tappan, of Ohio, on abolition petitions, delivered in Senate, February 4, 1840*.

[Tappan, Lewis.] *The Life of Arthur Tappan*. New York: Hurd and Houghton, 1870.

Thome, James A. *Emancipation in the West Indies, A six months' tour in Antigua, Barbadoes, and Jamaica, in the year 1837, by Jas. A. Thome, and J. Horace Kimball*. New York: American Anti-Slavery Society, 1838.

Thompson, George. *Prison Life and Reflection on, as Narrative of the Arrest, Trial, Conviction, Imprisonment, Treatment, Observa-*

tions, Reflections, and Deliverance of Work, Burr, and Thompson, who suffered as Unjust and Cruel Imprisonment in Missouri Penitentiary, for Attempting to Aid some Slaves to Liberty. 3 vols. in 1. 5th ed. Hartford: A. Work, 1850.

Thompson, Joseph Parrish. *Christianity and Emancipation, or, The Teachings and the Influence of the Bible Against Slavery.* New York: Anson D. F. Randolph, 1863.

Thomson, Mortimer. *Great Auction Sale of Slaves at Savannah, GA, March 2nd and 3rd, 1859, reported for the Tribune.* New York: American Anti-Slavery Society, 1859. Or *What Became of the Slaves on a Georgia Plantation?, Great Auction Sale of Slaves, at Savannah, GA, March 2d and 3d, 1859, a Sequel to Mrs. Kemble's Journal* [1863].

Townsend, Lucy. *"To the Law, and to the Testimony," or, Questions on Slavery Answered by the Scriptures, and presumed to be Worthy of Particular Consideration on the National Fast Day.* London: Hamilton, Adams, & Co., 1832.

Van Dyke, Henry Jackson. *The Character and Influence of Abolitionism, a sermon preached in the First Presbyterian Church, Brooklyn, on Sabbath evening, December 9, 1860, published by request.* New York: George F. Nesbitt & Co., 1860.

Washburn, Israel. *The Issues, the Dred Scott Decision, the Parties, speech of Hon. Israel Washburn, Jr., of Maine, delivered in the House of Representatives, May 19, 1860.* Washington: published by the Congressional Republican Committee, 1860.

———. *Speech of Hon. I. Washburn, Jr., of Maine, on the compromise as a national party test, delivered in the House of Representatives, May 24, 1852.* Washington: printed at the Congressional Globe Office, 1852.

Whipple, Charles King. *Slavery and the American Board of Commissioners for Foreign Missions.* New York: American Anti-Slavery Society, 1859.

Why Colored People in Philadelphia are Excluded from the Street Cars. Philadelphia: Merrihew & Son, printers, 1866.

Wilson, Henry. *History of the Antislavery Measures of the Thirty-seventh and Thirty-eighth United States Congresses, 1861-64.* Boston: Walker, Wise, and Company, 1864.

Yates, William. *Rights of Colored Men to Suffrage, Citizenship, and Trial by Jury, being a Book of Facts, Arguments and Authorities, Historical Notices and Sketches of Debates, with Notes.* Philadelphia: Merrihew & Gunn, 1838.

NOTES

[1] Copy given to the College in memory of **Henry Cheever**.

[2] The prefatory note to this pamphlet reads: "The Merit of originating the following treatise is due to **Ebenezer Dole**, a benevolent citizen of Hallowell, Maine, who, from a thorough conviction of the iniquity of slavery, and its utter inconsistency with the precepts of the gospel, was induced to remit fifty dollars to the Pennsylvania Society for promoting the Abolition of Slavery, & c. to be awarded to the writer of the best essay on the following subject: "The Duty of Ministers and Churchs, of all denominations, to avoid the stain of Slavery, and to make the holding of slaves a barrier to communion and church membership."

[3] Presented to the Athenaean Society by member Frederic Perley A.B. 1840 in 1837.

[4] The library's copy was formerly in the Athenaean Society library, donated by **John Albion Andrew** in 1837.

[5] Presented to the Peucinian Society in 1854 by Sophomores, including **William H. Smyth.**

[6] The library's copy of this volume was formerly owned by **William Pitt Fessenden** and given to him by Rev. S. S. Jocelyn, pastor of a black church in New Haven, in February 1866, and bears Jocelyn's autograph.

[7] Copy autographed "Presented by Claude L. Hemans," A.B. 1838, A.M. 1841.

[8] In same volume with George William Curtis, *Wendell Phillips.*

[9] Volume presented in remembrance of **Rev. Henry T. Cheever.**

[10] One copy given to Bowdoin College Library in memory of **Rev. Henry Cheever,** D. D., class of 1834.

[11] Presented to the Peucinian Society by the Class of 1860.

[12] Given to the Bowdoin College Library "In Grateful Remembrance of Rev. **Henry T. Cheever**, D.D."

Appendix C
Samuel and William Pitt Fessenden Letters

Correspondence relating to the slave issue between William Pitt Fessenden (WPF) and Samuel Fessenden (SF), from the Fessenden Papers.

SF to WPF, 7 July 1839, Portland.
WPF to SF, 15 February 1842, Washington, D.C.
WPF to SF, 29 September 1846, Portland.
WPF to SF, 8 March 1854, Washington, D.C.
SF to WPF, 17 May 1854, Portland.
SF to WPF, 6 June 1854, Portland.
SF to WPF, 6 January 1857, Portland.
SF to WPF, 10 April 1858, Portland.
WPF to SF, 23 December 1859, Washington, D.C.
WPF to SF, 16 February 1861, Washington, D.C.
SF to WPF, 16 March 1861, Portland.
SF to WPF with note from Charles Fessenden, 27 July 1861, Portland?
WPF to SF, 12 December 1861, Washington, D.C.
SF to WPF, 29 December 1861, Portland?
WPF to SF, 29 March 1862, Washington, D.C.
SF to WPF, 9 May 1862, Portland.
WPF to SF, 7 March 1864, Washington, D.C.
WPF to SF, 31 December 1865, Washington, D.C.

Alpheus Spring Packard (1798-1884), Class of 1816, Collins Professor of Natural and Revealed Religion, and Acting President.

John Parker Hale (1806-1873), Class of 1827.

William Pitt Fessenden (1806-1869), Class of 1823.

Bibliography

Anderson, Patricia. *The Architecture of Bowdoin College.* Brunswick, ME: Bowdoin College Museum of Art, 1988.

Beam, Philip C. *Winslow Homer's Magazine Engravings.* New York: Harper & Row, 1979.

Biographical Encyclopedia of Maine of the Nineteenth Century. Boston: Metropolitan Publishing & Engraving Company, 1885. (BEM)

Biographical Directory of the American Congress, 1774-1949. Washington, D.C.: Government Printing Office, 1950. (BDAC)

Biographical Directory of the Governors of the United States 1798-1978. Eds. Robert Sobel and John Raimo. Westport, CT: Meckler Books, 1978.

Clark, Calvin Montague. *American Slavery and Maine Congregationalists: A Chapter in the History of the Development of Anti-Slavery Sentiment in the Protestant Churches of the North.* Bangor, ME: By the Author, 1940. (Clark)

Cleaveland, Nehemiah. *History of Bowdoin College with Biographical Sketches of Its Graduates From 1806 to 1879 Inclusive.* Boston: James Ripley Osgood and Company, 1882. (Cleaveland)

Dictionary of Afro-American Slavery. Eds. Randall Miller and John David Smith. Westport, CT: Greenwood Press, 1988.

Dictionary of American Negro Biography. Eds. Rayford W. Logan and Michael R. Winston. New York: W. W. Norton & Co., 1982. (DANB)

Encyclopedia of World Biography. (EWB)

Fessenden, Allen Edwin. *The Fessenden Family in America*. Ed. Mary Wasburn. 1971. (Fessenden)

Genealogical and Family History of the State of Maine. Compiled by George Thomas Little. 4 vols. New York: Lewis Historical Publishing Company, 1909.

General Catalogue of Bowdoin College and the Medical School of Maine: A Biographical Record of Alumni and Officers, 1794-1950. Sesquicentennial Edition. Brunswick, ME: President and Trustees of Bowdoin College, 1950. (GCB)

Lamb's Biographical Dictionary of the United States. 7 vols. Boston: James H. Lamb Company, 1900-1903.

McGraw-Hill Encyclopedia of World Biography. 12 vols. New York: McGraw-Hill, 1973. (EWB)

Mallett, Richard P. "Maine Crusades and Crusaders 1830-1850." *Maine Historical Quarterly* 17 (1978):190-92.

Millet, Joshua. *A History of the Baptists in Maine; Together with Brief Notices of Societies and Institutions and a Dictionary of the Labors of Each Minister*. Portland [ME]: Charles Day & Co., 1845.

Nason, Emma Huntington. *Old Hallowell on the Kennebec*. Augusta, ME: Burleigh & Flynt, 1909. (Nason)

National Cyclopedia of American Biography. (NCAB)

North, James W. *History of Augusta from the Earliest Settlement to the Present Time: With Notices of the Plymouth Company and Settlements on the Kennebec; together with Biographical Sketches and Genealogical Register*. Augusta, ME: Clapp and North, 1870. (North)

Schriver, Edward O. "Abolitionists Organize: The Maine Antislavery Society." *Maine Historical Society Newsletter* 9 (1969). (Schriver 1969)

_____. *Go Free: The Antislavery Impulse in Maine, 1833-1855*. Orono, ME: University of Maine Press, 1970. (Schriver 1970)

Thurston, David. *A Brief History of Winthrop, From 1764 to October 1855*. Portland: Brown Thurston, 1855. (Thurston)

Warner, Ezra J. *Generals in Blue: Lives of the Union Commanders*. Louisiana State University Press, 1964. (Warner)

Who Was Who in America: Historical Volume, 1607-1896. Rev. ed. Chicago: Marquis, 1967. (WWWA)

Willey, Austin. *History of Antislavery in State and Nation*. Portland, ME: Brown Thurston & Hoy, Fogg, and Donham, 1886. (Willey)

Williamson, Joseph. A *Bibliography of the State of Maine, From the Earliest Period to 1891*. 2 vols. Portland, ME: The Thurston Print, 1896. (Williamson)

Index

BOWDOIN SUBJECTS

Adams, Aaron Chester	5, 38 n. 10
Adams, George Eliashib	61
Andrew, John Albion	5, 88 n. 4
Appleton, John	4, 6, 24 n. 1
Athenaean Society	xi, 27-28, 88 n. 3, 4
Blaine, James Gillespie	7, 24 n. 4, 48 n. 1
Bond, Elias	62
Bridge, Horatio	7, 9, 16
Cheever, George Barrell	8, 10, 24 n. 7
Cheever, Henry T.	9, 24 n. 7, 25 n. 8, 88 n. 1, 9, 10, 12
Chickering, John White	40, 62, 67 n. 1
Cummings, Asa	10, 28-29
Cutter, Edward Francis	10
Cutter, William	62-63
Davis, Woodbury	30, 37 n. 3
Dwight, William Theodore	21, 30-31, 38 n. 4
Eastman, Philip	10-11
Ellingwood, John Wallace	63
Fairfield, John	11, 25 n. 9, 45
Fessenden, Joseph Palmer	11-12
Fessenden, Samuel (b. 1784)	2, 12, 13, 31-32, 36, 38 n. 6 and 7, 45, 46, 56, 67 n. 1, 89
Fessenden, Samuel (b. 1841)	2, 4, 13
Fessenden, Samuel Clement	2, 12, 13
Fessenden, William Pitt	2, 12-13, 25 n. 12, 31, 88 n. 6, 89, 90
Freeman, Charles	13-14
Frye, William Pierce	7, 14
Gardiner, Robert Hallowell	37, 63, 67 n. 2
Gillet, Eliphalet	20, 32-33, 38 n. 8
Hale, John Parker	15, 90
Hall, James	15-16, 25 n. 13
Hawthorne, Nathaniel	8, 16
Holmes, Ezekiel	16-17
Holmes, John	33
Howard, Oliver Otis	xiii, 4, 7, 17, 40, 43, 54-59

Ladd, William	33-34
Longfellow, Henry Wadsworth	17-18, 25 n. 14, 43
Lovejoy, Joseph Cammet	44, 64, 67 n. 3
Lovejoy, Owen	18
Nichols, Icabod	64, 67 n. 4
Packard, Alpheus Spring	4, 18-19, 39, 61, 62, 90
Parris, Albion Keith	64-65
Peucinian Society	xi, 4, 27-28, 88 n. 5, 11
Pickard, Samuel	65
Prentiss, George Lewis	19
Pomeroy, Swan L.	34-35, 42
Rice, Richard Drury	35-36
Russwurm, John Brown	vi, xi, 4, 8, 15, 19-20, 25 n. 15
Shepard, Rev. George	20
Smyth, Egbert C.	20-21, 25 n. 16, 38 n. 4
Smyth, William	3, 4, 18, 21-22, 45, 60, 62, 63, 88 n. 5
Stone, Thomas Treadwell	22
Stowe, Calvin Ellis	42, 43, 65-66, 67 n. 5, 6, and 7
Tappan, Benjamin	66-67
Tenney, John Searle	23, 68
Thurston, David	5, 21, 36-37, 38 n. 10, 47, 93
Upham, Thomas Cogswell	39, 60, 63
Vose, Richard Hampton	23
Woods, Leonard	37, 38 n. 11, 61, 63, 68

NON-BOWDOIN SUBJECTS

Abbott, Lyman	48-53, 59 n. 3, 66
Ames, Adelbert	54
Appleton, James	61-62
Beecher, Henry Ward	43, 54-55, 66
Bellows, Henry	49
Bigelow, John	49-50
Chaplin, Jeremiah	47
Chase, Salmon Portland	55, 75
Conway, Moncure	50
Conway, Thomas	54, 55-56
Dole, Ebenezer, Sr.	20, 43, 44, 48 n. 4, 88 n. 2
Douglass, Frederick	1, 17, 32, 43, 56, 59 n. 4, 77
Douglass, Frederick, Jr.	56
DuBois, William E. B.	50

Fisk, Clinton B. 56-57
Garnet, Henry Highland 57
Garrison, William Lloyd...............................7, 12, 20, 24 n. 7, 31, 32, 38 n. 10, 42, 43, 44, 46, 47, 48 n. 4, 50-51, 59 n. 2, 64, 67 n. 4, 77-78
Greeley, Horace 51
Hale, Edward E. 57
Hamlin, Hannibal..17, 45, 48 n. 5
Ketchum, Edgar 57
Merwin, C. H. 57-58
Perry, John Jasiel 45-46
Saxton, Rufus 51, 54, 58
Severance, Luther ....7, 41, 48 n. 1
Seward, William H. 51-52
Sherman, William Tecumseh 52
Speer, Emery 52
Stowe, Harriet Beecher ....17, 42-43, 48 n. 3, 65, 67 n. 5
Sumner, Charles..58
Truth, Sojourner 17, 58-59
Tupper, Martin Farquhar 53
Washington, Booker T. ....50, 53, 59 n. 3
Willey, Rev. Austin ....xii, 44, 45, 67 n. 1, 93

Notes on Contributors

STUDENTS

Kristin L. Hall '91 will enter Washington University School of Law, St. Louis, Missouri, after completing a summer internship at the Smithsonian Institution in Washington, D.C.

Gregory J. Hostetter '91 double majored in Latin American studies and history. He plans to work as a crew member aboard a schooner sailing in the British and American Virgin Islands before pursuing graduate studies in history.

Michael E. Libonati '91 will work with the Colorado State Environmental Agency in Boulder and for the U. S. House of Representatives Office of the Sergeant at Arms in Washington, D.C., in the fall.

Daniel J. Lind '91 majored in Afro-American studies and history with a minor in women's studies. He will enter the master's program in Africana at Cornell University in the fall of 1991.

Bruce C. Moses '91 is entertaining a short stint aboard an Alaskan salmon ship before teaching English in Japanese primary schools.

John R. Nicholson, Jr. '91 double majored in history and religion.

Harriet H. Richards '92 is a dual major in anthropology and history. She is one of Bowdoin's nontraditional students, having returned to college after raising a family of four children. In addition to her role as a student, she serves as the administrative assistant to the director of the Africana Studies Program.

Sharma J. Simmons '94 plans to declare a double major in history (with a concentration on Medieval and Renaissance European studies) and art history. Upon receipt of an A.B., she intends to pursue a law degree with emphasis on corporate or criminal law.

COVER ARTIST

Thomas C. Killion (Ph.D, Stanford) is assistant professor of African history in the Department of History at Bowdoin College. Wood engraving is his avocation, and he has published two books of his art.

EDITOR

Angela M. Leonard, consortium dissertation fellow and lecturer in history at Bowdoin College for the 1990-1991 academic year, holds an A.B. *cum laude* from Harvard/Radcliffe Colleges, an M.L.S. from Peabody College of Vanderbilt University, and an M.Phil. from the George Washington University, where she is also completing a Ph.D. in American studies. She has published bibliographic aids for Howard and Fisk universities.